SECRETS

of the

NATURAL RESOURCE
MARKET

HOW TO SET YOURSELF UP FOR HUGE RETURNS IN MINING, ENERGY, AND AGRICULTURE

By Stansberry & Associates

Published by Stansberry & Associates Investment Research

Edited by Fawn Gwynallen

About Stansberry & Associates

Founded in 1999 and based out of Baltimore, Maryland, Stansberry & Associates Investment Research is the largest independent source of financial insight in the world. It delivers unbiased investment advice to self-directed investors seeking an edge in a wide variety of sectors and market conditions.

S&A has nearly two dozen analysts and researchers – including former hedge-fund managers and buy-side financial experts. They produce a steady stream of timely research on value investing, income generation, resources, biotech, financials, short-selling, macroeconomic analysis, options trading, and more.

The company's unrelenting and uncompromised insight has made it one of the most respected and sought-after research organizations in the financial sector. It has nearly one million readers and more than 500,000 paid subscribers in over 100 countries.

About the Contributors

Matt Badiali

 Matt Badiali is the editor of the *S&A Resource Report*, a monthly advisory focused on investments in energy, metals, and other natural resources. Over the years, Matt has recorded an incredible list of triple-digit winners, like Northern Dynasty Minerals (322%), Silver Wheaton (345%), and Jinshan Gold Mines (339%), among many others.

Matt takes a "boots on the ground" approach to his research. His work has taken him to Papua New Guinea, Iraq, Hong Kong, Singapore, Haiti, Turkey, Switzerland, and many other locations around the world. He has built a huge Rolodex of the most influential people in the industry – from private financiers, leading geologists, and natural-resource analysts to billionaire hedge-fund managers.

Prior to joining Stansberry & Associates Investment Research in 2005, Matt was a geologist for a drilling company and a consultant to an environmental company. He has appeared on Fox Business, Stansberry Radio, and other business news programs. He is also a regular contributor to *The Energy Report* and *Growth Stock Wire*.

Porter Stansberry

Porter Stansberry founded Stansberry & Associates Investment Research in 1999 with the firm's flagship newsletter, *Stansberry's Investment Advisory*. He is also the host of Stansberry Radio, a weekly podcast that is one of the most popular online financial radio shows.

Prior to launching S&A, Porter was the first American editor of the *Fleet Street Letter*, the world's oldest English-language financial newsletter.

Porter is well-known for doing some of the most important – and often controversial – work in the financial advisory business. Since he launched *Stansberry's Investment Advisory*, his string of accurate forecasts has made his newsletter one of the most widely read in the world... and has helped his readers both avoid catastrophe and make incredible gains.

Brian Hunt

Brian Hunt is the Editor in Chief of Stansberry & Associates.

Since 2007, he has managed dozens of S&A's investment newsletters and trading advisories, helping make S&A one of the largest financial publishers in the world.

Brian is a successful private trader and frequently contributes to *Growth Stock Wire*, *DailyWealth*, and *The S&A Digest*. He is the co-founder of *DailyWealth Trader*, one of the world's most popular and highly-regarded trading advisories.

Brian is also the co-author of the book *High Income Retirement: How to Safely Earn 12%-20% Income Streams on Your Savings*.

Dr. Steve Sjuggerud

Dr. Steve Sjuggerud is the editor of *True Wealth*, which focuses on safe, unique, alternative investments overlooked by Wall Street. He is also the editor of *True Wealth Systems*, which has distilled decades of Steve's investing experience into three dozen computer trading models.

Prior to joining S&A in 2001, Steve was a stockbroker, vice president of a global mutual fund, and head of a hedge fund. He has been quoted by the *Wall Street Journal*, *Barron's*, and the *Washington Post*. He also co-authored *Safe Strategies for Financial Freedom*, a bestselling book on investment strategies. He holds a doctorate in finance.

Guest Contributors

Rick Rule

 Rick Rule is the founder and chairman of Global Resource Investments, now a member of the Sprott Group of companies. Sprott Global Resource Investments provides investment advice and management, as well as brokerage services to high-net-worth individuals, institutional investors, and corporate entities worldwide.

Rick began his career in the securities business in 1974. He is a well-recognized expert in mining, energy, water, forest products, infrastructure, and agriculture. He has also financed several of the most important resource companies in the world. Rick is a frequent speaker at industry conferences and is often interviewed on radio, television, print, and online media outlets, including Business News Network, CNBC, and King World News.

John Doody

John Doody is the founder and editor of *Gold Stock Analyst*, which features his proprietary gold-stock valuing system. From 2001 to 2010, his "Top 10" list of gold stocks returned 1,360%.

Prior to launching *Gold Stock Analyst*, John received a BA in Economics from Columbia University, an MBA in finance, and a PhD in economics from Boston University. He was an economics professor for almost two decades.

But for the past 40 years, John has been studying and analyzing gold stocks. His opinion on these stocks is so respected, he has been profiled by *Barron's* several times, quoted in *The Financial Times*, and is frequently interviewed on CNBC. He counts several of the world's best-known gold funds and investment managers among his subscribers.

Table of Contents

Foreword

By Brian Hunt

"You're either a contrarian or a victim."

I heard those words more than 10 years ago.

It was an art and a science, summed up in just seven words.

That summary was worth hundreds of millions of dollars.

The words were spoken by one of the smartest, most successful people I've ever met, Rick Rule.

Rick is one of the top natural resource investors in history. As the founder of Global Resource Investments Limited (now part of Sprott Asset Management), Rick has made hundreds of millions of dollars for himself and his clients.

Rick is a walking encyclopedia of investment knowledge... especially when it relates to the extraction of natural resources like crude oil, gold, silver, copper, and uranium.

Over the past four decades, Rick has done deals with the world's most powerful people. He's been all over the world analyzing natural resource projects. Ask him a question about something like gold mining or oil drilling, and you might get a 30-minute answer that provides you with a Masters-level education on your chosen topic.

Despite everything Rick has done... despite all his experience and knowledge... he can boil down his extraordinary success to seven words:

"You're either a contrarian or a victim."

Making a fortune in natural resources is really that simple...

You buy assets when the public can't stand the thought of buying them (when the assets are cheap)... and make a fortune.

Or you buy assets when they are extremely popular (when the assets are expensive)... and lose.

"You're either a contrarian or a victim" is simple, yet powerful. Take detailed economic reports, extensive geologic data, and expensive political analysis and throw it all in the garbage. None of it will help you successfully invest in natural resources if you don't understand "contrarian or victim."

"Contrarian or victim" is the core idea of the book you're currently reading. It's the path to making money in one of the most potentially lucrative sectors of the entire stock market: natural resources.

This is the area of the market where oil-exploration firms can shoot 1,500% higher when they discover large new fields... and where gold stocks can climb 500% in just a few years on a surge in the gold price.

The rewards in the sector can be large. **But so can the risks**.

Too many people miss the contrarian mark and end up as victims.

For every one story of someone making a bundle in these stocks, there are dozens of stories of people losing big.

In the pages that follow, you'll receive a world-class education on natural resources. You'll learn from natural-resource experts like Rick Rule, Matt Badiali, and John Doody.

You'll learn how to be a contrarian instead of a victim. You'll learn about several unique business models that often produce huge wins. You'll learn the professional's "back door" way to profiting from natural-resource booms... and dozens of other tips.

The natural resource sector is full of big rewards and big risks. The people who reap the rewards are called "contrarians." The people who get burned by the risks are called "victims."

This guide will ensure you wear the "contrarian" label... and reap the rewards that come with it.

Regards,

Brian Hunt
Editor in Chief
Stansberry & Associates

A Quick Introduction to Natural Resource Investment

By Brian Hunt

Before we begin, let's answer an important question...

"What is natural resource investment?"

Natural resource investment is the investment in the use or the extraction of Earth's raw materials.

It is investing in the "building blocks" of civilization.

It's a big, broad topic... with lots of different angles. Investing in natural resources includes:

- Oil and natural gas wells
- Copper mines
- Gold mines
- Coal mines
- Iron ore mines
- Timberland
- Farmland
- Fertilizer
- Water
- Livestock
- Gravel pits

That's a lot of angles. And those are just the "major" ones.

But generally, the natural resource sector can be broken down into four "common sense" groupings.

Keep in mind, other folks use other groupings.

Below is just how we at Stansberry & Associates like to view them...

Energy

The energy group consists of crude oil, natural gas, gasoline, coal, heating oil, and uranium.

A common-sense description of this group is, *"The stuff we burn to heat our homes, produce electricity, and fuel our vehicles."*

Most of the world's energy comes from "fossil fuels." Fossil fuels come from the remains of organisms that died hundreds of thousands of years ago.

Fossil fuels like crude oil and natural gas are used to produce gasoline, chemicals, plastics, motor oil, and fertilizer.

Uranium is sort of the "odd man out" in the energy group. Uranium isn't a fossil fuel. When refined, it's a metal. When uranium is broken down, it emits huge amounts of energy. This has made it a component of weapons... and the chief fuel for nuclear power plants.

Precious Metals

The precious-metals group consists of gold, silver, platinum, and palladium.

A common-sense description of this group is, *"The metals people typically find beautiful to look at... and to use for money."*

Gold and silver have been used as jewelry for centuries. They are also useful forms of money. Nations and individuals stockpile gold as a form of wealth and power.

As civilization has progressed, we've found many other uses for precious metals. Silver is used to make medical tools and electronics. Platinum and palladium are used to make catalytic converters, which reduce air pollution from automobiles.

Base Metals and Construction Aggregates

If you think of precious metals as the metals humans like to look at, you can think of "base" metals as the metals humans don't particularly like to look at.

A common-sense description of this group is, *"The metals and rocks people like to use when building stuff."*

The base metals and construction aggregate group tends to be the useful "building blocks" of modern civilization. It includes copper, iron ore, tin, aluminum, nickel, zinc, lead, gravel, and dozens of other lesser-known minerals and metals.

Metals like copper and zinc aren't used much in jewelry. But they're widely used in building power lines, skyscrapers, bridges, cars, trucks, bulldozers, and railroads.

Agriculture

This is the resource group that grows. It includes corn, soybeans, wheat, coffee, cocoa, cotton, cattle, hogs, oats, rice, sugar, orange juice, and lumber.

A common-sense description of this group is, *"The things we grow for food and building materials."*

You'll note that most of these agricultural products are turned into food. However, a few members of the agriculture group are used for other purposes, like lumber (building houses) and cotton (clothing and fabric).

When traders talk about the agriculture group, they often break it into smaller groups, like "grains" (corn, soybeans, wheat), "softs" (orange juice, sugar, cocoa), and "meat" (cattle and hogs).

For our general purposes in this book though, we'll classify agriculture as the stuff that is grown... not drilled or mined.

Now that you have an idea of what natural resources are and how they are grouped, you're ready to learn the most important rules of resource investing...

— Part 1—

The *S&A Resource Report* Guide to Investing in Natural Resource Stocks

By Matt Badiali, editor, *S&A Resource Report*

— Part 1 —

The *S&A Resource Report* Guide to Investing in Natural Resource Stocks

By Matt Badiali, editor, *S&A Resource Report*

On January 18, 2002, shares of the world's largest publicly traded uranium producer, Cameco, traded for just $3.37 per share.

Five years later, Cameco shares traded for $50 per share... a 1,483% increase in value.

On Valentine's Day 2001, shares of Goldcorp, one of the world's premier gold miners, traded for just $2.50 per share.

Seven years later, Goldcorp shares traded for $53 per share... a 2,000% increase in value.

In March 2003, shares of Potash Corp, one of the world's premier fertilizer miners, traded for $3 per share.

Seven years later, Potash traded for $75 per share... a 2,400% increase in value.

To give you an idea of the wealth-creating potential of these gains, realize that a 2,400% return on a $10,000 investment results in a stake valued at $250,000.

These are the types of gains investors can realize when they make great investments based on the cycles of natural resources.

Although many people understand how lucrative these markets can be, most don't understand how they work. In fact, most investors who deal in this sector are constant losers.

This guide will teach you the key to investing in the natural resource sector. This "key" is so important that if you don't thoroughly understand it, nothing else you do right can possibly help you.

If you do understand this key, and several other useful concepts contained in this guide, you can profitably trade the natural resource sector for the rest of your life.

Remember... investing and speculating in natural resources can be incredibly risky. It's simply too volatile an area for conservative investors.

But if you're willing to speculate in resources, there are three important things to keep in mind...

1. Understand the role of cyclicality.
2. Study all the tools at your disposal to determine your risk.
3. Follow an established exit strategy.

These are the keys to making a fortune in resource stocks. We'll discuss each in this section.

We'll also look at the most important number in natural resources and the most dangerous thing a resource investor will encounter.

The first lesson we'll look at in Chapter 1 is how to master the booms and busts of the resource sector... (Hint: It's all about the trend.)

— 1 —

How to Master the Booms and Busts of the Resource Sector

One aspect of the resource business is so important that if you don't thoroughly understand it, nothing else you do right can possibly help you.

You will lose every cent you put here.

Insiders call this aspect *"cyclicality."*

Cyclicality might sound like industry-speak, but it's actually a simple concept... A cyclical asset is one that booms and busts like crazy.

One year, it will skyrocket 200%... The next year, it will plunge 50%. After plunging, it might drift sideways for a year, and then rise 300%.

Contrast this to a "noncyclical" asset, like shares of Johnson & Johnson (JNJ)...

JNJ is the world's largest health care and consumer-products company. It sells everyday items like Listerine, Tylenol, and Band-Aids. Demand for these products is relatively constant. Even recessions do little to dent mouthwash sales. This makes JNJ shares relatively noncyclical. They don't go through wild booms and busts.

Natural resources, however, do go through wild booms and busts. Consider the case of uranium from 2000 to 2008...

Uranium is a natural resource whose chief use is fueling nuclear-power reactors. For much of the 1990s, uranium prices were mired in a bear market. Excess supplies from the previous years depressed prices.

Low prices meant no one was investing in new uranium deposits. There simply wasn't any money in it.

In 2003, for example, it cost miners $20 per pound to mine uranium, but they were selling it for $15 per pound. Miners were *losing* about $5 on every pound of uranium they produced. Mines closed, and no new ones opened.

It was grim – a classic "bust."

Then... after years of bust... we started seeing increased demand for the cheap fuel. But the lack of investment in new uranium projects meant supply was limited. Increased demand and low supply pushed uranium prices higher and higher.

As you can see from the chart below, prices quadrupled in about three years...

Uranium

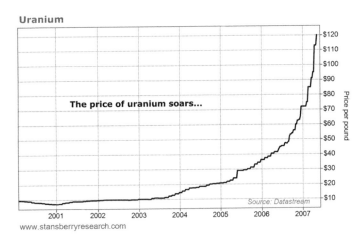

The price of uranium soars...

Source: Datastream

www.stansberryresearch.com

In response to this new uranium boom, exploration companies went wild. The table below shows uranium exploration spending in Canada (a major uranium-producing country). You can see how fast the industry increased spending...

Year	Uranium Exploration Investment
2003	$2.5 million
2004	$9.5 million
2005	$53.9 million
2006	$124.5 million
2007	$139.6 million

Data from OECD/IAEA

That's an incredible 5,484% increase in uranium-exploration investment in just four years.

This shows you that when a commodity goes into a "boom" cycle, it attracts huge amounts of money. Uranium climbed from $10 per pound in 2002 to nearly $140 per pound five years later.

You can imagine what that kind of rise does to the share price of companies in the sector...

Consider junior uranium explorer Mega Uranium (MGA). Its ride from 2003 to 2007 was spectacular. Shares went from $0.04 each in September 2003 to $7.41 in April 2007. That's an amazing 18,425% return...

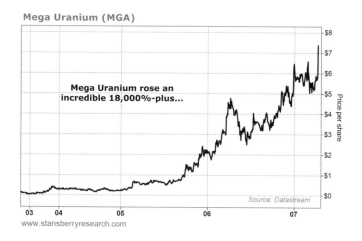

Mega Uranium (MGA)

Mega Uranium rose an incredible 18,000%-plus...

Source: Datastream

www.stansberryresearch.com

Now remember... every "boom" eventually turns to "bust."

In any given resource sector, *the cure for high prices is high prices.*

When huge amounts of money flow into a sector, it creates tons of new companies, bloated values, increased supplies, and eventually, plunging prices.

Hundreds of new uranium-exploration companies were created from 2004 to 2007 to capitalize on the new uranium boom... many with no real assets or even a hope of becoming a real company.

As you can see from the updated chart of uranium (on the next page), the boom turned to bust. Uranium prices collapsed from nearly $140 per pound to $40 per pound...

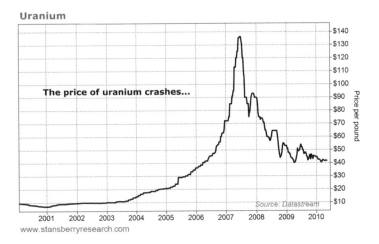

Uranium

The price of uranium crashes...

Source: Datastream

www.stansberryresearch.com

Most uranium stocks lost more than 90% of their value. Shares of Mega Uranium peaked at $7.41 in April 2007 and had fallen to $0.37 by June 2010. That's a 95% decline in three years...

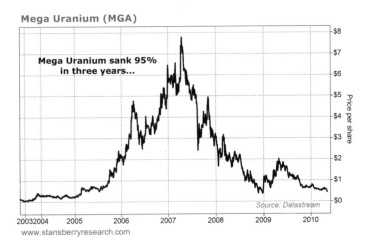

Mega Uranium (MGA)

Mega Uranium sank 95% in three years...

Source: Datastream

www.stansberryresearch.com

Investors lost $0.95 of every $1 they invested if they followed the crowd, bought at the top, and didn't cut their losses.

It's not just uranium. These cycles happen all the time in natural resources. Oil, natural gas, nickel, copper, platinum... you name it. Commodities boom and bust like crazy.

When "bust" periods of excess supply depress prices, people find new uses for the cheap resource. At the same time, producers of that resource can't make much money, so they stop investing in new projects to bring on supplies.

This "*increased demand, decreased supply*" situation creates a crunch that drives prices up by hundreds of percent... and causes incredible stock gains in the companies that focus on that resource.

Then, after prices rise, increased supplies come online... Producers of that resource invest heavily in new projects to cash in on the "boom" times.

Meanwhile, users of the now-expensive resource look for alternatives. This decreases demand.

The "*decreased demand, increased supply*" situation can crush the price of the commodity... and send the share prices of stocks that focus on that resource down more than 90%.

All commodities are highly cyclical. And while these big cycles chew up most crowd-following investors, you can use them to make incredible profits in mining, agriculture, and energy stocks.

You simply get into booms early and avoid the big busts.

My friend Rick Rule is one of the greatest resource investors in the world. He has made himself and his clients hundreds of millions of dollars with his ability to spot great values, get into big resource trends early, and avoid big resource busts.

He coined the phrase, "*You're either a contrarian or a victim.*"

Rick's phrase captures everything you need to know about resource trends. To make huge gains, you have to buy assets when nobody wants them – like uranium stocks in the late 1990s. This is when assets get very cheap.

Going against the crowd in these situations will give you a sick feeling in your gut.

But that's a sign that you're probably doing the right thing.

When the crowd wakes up to the boom times that follow the bust, they'll bid up your shares to incredible heights. That's when you – the contrarian – sell out to the unfortunate victim.

That's the way to make big money in resources. It has been the case for hundreds of years... and it will be the case for hundreds more.

More than any other sector, natural resources can produce gains of 100%, 500%, or even 1,000%.

But you have to know what you're doing. And you have to have the right tools for the job...

An Essential Toolkit for Resource Investors

You realize that to succeed as a commodity investor, you must master the resource cycle.

You know "you're either a contrarian or a victim."

And let's say you've found a specific sector – like gold or oil – that allows you to take advantage of contrarian bargains.

Now you need to "get long." And the decision you have to make is what tool to use for the job.

There are several ways to make a bullish bet on a commodity. Each has its pros and cons... its particular risks and rewards. One investment might be a great idea for some folks, but terrible for others.

I'll show you how to choose...

When it comes to resources, we can put our trading "tools" in nine broad categories.

I'll give you a "thumbnail" overview of each category and grade its risk as low, moderate, or high.

Remember though, investing in natural resources is inherently riskier than most sectors. So a low-risk natural resource investment is likely far riskier than a big blue-chip stock. (Only experienced traders who can handle volatility should even consider putting money in anything high-risk.)

One more note before we begin: *These ratings are specific to the resource market...* I'm not considering how risky any of these categories are relative to bonds, real estate, or blue-chip stocks, for example.

Let's get started on the "low risk" end...

RISK RATING: LOW

The Physical

"If you're bullish on a given commodity and you have the means, just buy the stuff!"

That's the advice you'll hear from investors who don't want to trade in and out of stocks.

The problem is... most commodities don't lend themselves to low-cost, efficient storage.

Sure, you can buy 10 ounces of gold bullion and store it in a vault. But most folks don't have the means to store corn, crude oil, natural gas, uranium, or cotton.

Generally, buying the physical commodity itself only works with precious metals like gold, silver, and platinum. They have tremendous "value density" – just a handful of one-ounce coins can add up to $10,000.

So owning a stash of gold, silver, and platinum coins is a great idea, in my opinion. It's real, tangible wealth to keep on hand in case of a dollar crisis... or if you need to discreetly transfer a large amount of wealth.

Price risk is our main concern when owning the physical product.

RISK RATING: LOW

The "Biggies"

In any given commodity sector, there are usually a handful of giant producers that dominate the industry.

They have the money to hire most of the best people, they manage the biggest projects, they buy the most equipment, and their capital spending "sets the tone" for the rest of the industry.

In the gold sector, for example, a handful of large producers mine most of the world's gold. These include Barrick, Goldcorp, Newmont, AngloGold Ashanti, and Newcrest.

In the oil sector, you have ExxonMobil, Royal Dutch Shell, and Chevron (in addition to large, state-owned companies that aren't publicly traded).

The "biggies" typically have been around a long time and have fairly stable businesses. They have a mix of assets around the world. Their market caps are anywhere from $10 billion to $300 billion (depending on the industry). Many pay dividends.

This means they are less volatile than smaller companies... and are appropriate for conservative investors.

They are not without risk, however. A big fall in the price of the commodity they produce can send their shares lower. Likewise, shares might stall if increases in their costs of production outpace increases in the price of the commodity they produce.

RISK RATING: MODERATE

Exchange-Traded Funds, Part 1

When it comes to resource investing, exchange-traded funds (ETFs) come in two different "flavors"...

The lowest-risk group owns diversified baskets of companies. For example, the iShares U.S. Energy Sector Fund (IYE) owns a broad swath of oil producers, explorers, and various other energy firms. In mid-2014, the fund owned 86 different energy stocks.

When it comes to gold, a popular fund is the Market Vectors Gold Miners Fund (GDX). In mid-2014, this fund owned 40 different gold stocks, some large, some small.

When you own a diversified basket of stocks, you give up much of your upside. You'll also end up owning lots of "so-so" companies. But these ETFs can give you exposure to a sector without subjecting you to the risk of owning just one or two companies. These are appropriate for risk averse investors.

RISK RATING: MODERATE

Royalty Firms

This is one of my favorite categories. Royalty companies are a unique and efficient way to invest in a given resource trend.

Most royalty companies are in the gold and silver sector. But they mine no metals of their own. Instead, they finance a lot of early-stage exploration or production projects. When a mine they finance starts producing, the royalty company gets a cut of the cash flow.

Royalty companies are high-profit-margin, diversified, and leveraged ways to speculate on higher commodity prices. The large royalty firm Royal Gold, for example, climbed 23-fold from mid-2001 to 2011. The large silver royalty firm, Silver Wheaton, climbed 14-fold from its credit-crisis low in 2008 to its 2011 high.

If you buy quality royalty firms when their underlying commodities are out of favor, you can set yourself up for huge gains. But always keep in mind that their share prices can fall if the price of their underlying commodity falls or if there is a problem with their projects.

RISK RATING: MODERATE

Picks and Shovels

Another one of my favorite ways to invest in a resource boom is with "picks and shovels." These companies provide vital equipment and services needed to explore for and extract resources.

The classic "picks and shovels" success story is set in the 1850s. Back then, a German immigrant moved from New York to San Francisco to participate in the California Gold Rush.

Rather than the "all or nothing" route of looking for a big gold strike, this guy sold basic goods to the miners. He eventually started producing a new type of durable pants. They became a huge hit... and he got rich.

His name was Levi Strauss. Levi didn't risk it all on trying to find the big strike, he just sold the stuff everyone else needed to try to find the next big strike themselves.

The idea of owning "picks and shovels" has become an investment cliché for good reason. It can be an incredibly profitable, diversified way to profit from rising commodity prices.

When it comes to modern-day picks and shovels, we have a wide variety of ideas to consider...

You have companies like Schlumberger and Halliburton. These two companies are giant "oil service" providers. They sell equipment and services to large oil companies...

You have Joy Global, which sells mining equipment... You have Core Laboratories, which performs advanced seismic research so oil companies know where to drill... You have companies like Trican Well

Services and Calfrac that perform the new type of "hydraulic fracturing" services that have revolutionized North American energy production...

You have Kennametal, which sells extremely durable cutting teeth and blades to explorers... You have Bristow Group, which sells helicopter services to the offshore oil and gas industry.

The variety of picks-and-shovels choices is extraordinary. And one well-timed buy when these companies are out of favor can make for hundreds of percent gains. But always keep in mind that these companies boom when times are good and bust when times are not so good.

RISK RATING: MODERATE

The Mid-Tier Producers

You can consider "mid-tier" producers as "biggies in training."

Mid-tier producers are still relatively large companies, with market caps ranging from $1 billion to $50 billion (again, depending on the industry). But mid-tier producers typically have a narrower asset base.

For example, a gold-mining "biggie" might operate 10 large mines around the world. A mid-tier producer might operate just two or three large mines.

Because mid-tier producers have less asset diversification, they are riskier than larger, more diversified companies. If a mid-tier producer has a major problem with one of its mines or oilfields, it will cause a huge swing in its profitability and a huge swing in its share price.

Commodity price changes cause these stocks to move, as well. For example, a 10% change in commodity price (gold, silver, oil, etc) can make a huge difference in profits. So a small fall in the commodity price can have a big impact on the share price. That's why these companies have a higher risk rating.

RISK RATING: HIGH

Exchange-Traded Funds, Part 2

The other "flavor" of resource ETFs is option funds.

These funds trade directly in their given resource, instead of through shares (like gold fund GDX). They trade futures contracts to attempt to track the price of the commodity.

A futures contract is a written agreement between a buyer and seller of any commodity. The agreement specifies what is going to be sold, for how much, and when it will be delivered.

There are funds that rise and fall in lockstep with gold and silver prices, for example. There are funds that attempt to rise and fall with oil, natural gas, and copper prices.

I'm generally not a fan of these funds. Most of them "bleed" value because the futures cost money... and the funds typically charge substantial fees.

Also, when it comes to owning "real money" assets like gold and silver, why own "digital" when you can own the real stuff?

RISK RATING: HIGH

Nonproducers With Good Assets

"Nonproducers with good assets" is an odd class of resource stock.

These are companies that own one or two large assets that could be turned into mines or oilfields... but for some reason or another, have not been put into production.

Seabridge Gold is one of the highest-profile companies in this class. It owns the "KSM" project in British Columbia, Canada. KSM is one of the world's largest undeveloped gold and copper deposits. It's an absolute monster, with nearly 40 million ounces of gold and 10 billion pounds of copper in proven and probable reserves.

The problem with KSM is that it's in an inaccessible area of Canada. Huge investments in roads and electrical infrastructure are required to mine KSM. We're talking billions of dollars. Still, if gold prices were to soar, it would be worth it.

You can profit from these types of plays if you buy them when their underlying commodities are in the pits... and on the cusp of a big rally. From 2005 to 2008, for example, Seabridge Gold rallied more than 1,000%.

But investors have to be very careful buying these companies. Often, these big deposits have big factors working against them... like environmental concerns, political concerns, or, in Seabridge's case, a remote location. They are among the riskiest plays in the resource market.

RISK RATING: HIGH

Junior Explorers

Junior explorers are the "bloodhounds" of the resource industry.

Their market caps are typically in the $5 million-$100 million range, miniscule next to a "biggie." (ExxonMobil is 1,000 times larger than a $38 million "junior.")

The business model here is to find a prospective area that could be rich in metals or oil, raise money from investors, hire geologists and some drilling equipment, and look for a big strike. If it finds that big strike, the junior will sell it to a larger company.

Early investors can make 1,000%... 5,000%... even 10,000% here. But this is the "Wild West" of the resource stock world. Junior explorers are the riskiest area of the market. They are inappropriate for 99.9% of investors. They have little in the way of tangible assets. They are essentially a group of corporate managers and geologists with a dream and a story.

The vast majority burn up their cash and find nothing.

In any given industry, however, there are some folks who are habitually successful when it comes to finding big resource deposits. If you stick to investing with proven, honest managers, you can make great money in "juniors."

Just keep in mind that out of a random selection of 1,000 junior explorers, just five or 10 are worth considering as a speculation.

Again, **most investors should steer clear of this market**, which has less trading liquidity and lots of worthless companies masquerading as "investments."

Toolbox Summary

When it comes to "playing" a resource trend, you have lots of tools. You have to decide for yourself how much risk and volatility you can tolerate.

In the *S&A Resource Report*, we invest in the a mix of "biggies," mid-tier producers, royalty firms, the physical, selected funds, and picks and shovels.

I avoid most "pure play" funds. I only recommend "juniors" to folks who are comfortable with handling risk and volatility.

You might note that I've left futures and options off this list. I know many folks who are successful in these areas of the market, but it's totally inappropriate for most individual investors. Please only swim in these waters if you are an advanced trader.

But even for advanced traders, understanding the tools of the trade will get you nowhere if you don't develop a method to reduce your risk and maximize your gains in the market. You need an exit strategy. So let's take a look at a great way to preserve your gains in the resource market...

— 3 —

How to 'Ring the Cash Register' With Resource Stocks

Not one man saw the bloodshed that was coming...

In the summer of 2008, I spent three weeks in Vancouver. The city is home to the thousands of junior resource companies that trade on the Toronto Stock Exchange Venture Index (TSX V), the "Dow Jones of small resource stocks."

While I was there, I spoke to dozens of industry insiders, geologists, and mining company executives. These are the sector "insiders." Many of them make their living speculating in junior mining stocks...

But no one knew what was coming...

By December of that year – six months later – *the TSX V had dropped nearly 75%*.

Most resource stock owners were caught with their pants down. They didn't have an exit strategy in place. They should have booked big gains and cut their losses early. Instead, they watched millions of dollars in profits evaporate... and rode their stocks all the way down.

Often, resource investors are their own worst enemies. They'll sell winners too early to lock in fast gains... or they'll hold on to a loser because of hope or the reluctance to admit they were wrong about a position.

But "hope" doesn't qualify as a selling plan.

Fortunately, there's a simple system you can use with your resource trades that will both reduce your risk and maximize your returns.

Let me show you how it works with an example...

Back in late 2009, I recommended buying shares of a promising gold explorer, ATAC Resources.

"Juniors" like ATAC are the bloodhounds of the resource business. They are tiny companies that scour the world looking for the next big deposit.

When one of them finds a huge deposit, shares absolutely skyrocket.

But that kind of potential doesn't come without risk. So we had a "sell" strategy starting from the first day we bought it.

In this case, I set a 50% trailing stop. We were prepared to lose half our investment before we sold. The huge potential reward made up for that level of risk.

The rewards came quickly. We made a 70% initial gain in the first three months.

Many investors (particularly those without a plan) would have taken that cash off the table right then and there. They'd be ecstatic with a 70% gain in three months.

But I knew the 2010 drilling season hadn't even begun. I knew that initial return was just other investors hearing the story and getting excited. The big potential was still coming. So I kept my 50% trailing stop in place (in case I was wrong) and sat back to watch.

By mid-July, we had a 125% gain. Again, there was that temptation to lock in gains... But I knew only half of the drilling program was complete, less than one-quarter of the analysis on the drill cores was done. So we continued to hold.

By late August, drilling confirmed ATAC had discovered a major new gold deposit in the Yukon. The company's shares suddenly grew wings and soared.

They rocketed from $1.85 on August 19 to $7.22 on September 7.

As the stock rose, we tightened our trailing stop.

A trailing stop is easy to figure. For example, if a stock's highest closing price is $10 and you set a 25% trailing stop, you'd exit the stock if it declined below $7.50 (25% of $10 is $2.50, $10 minus $2.50 is $7.50).

A trailing stop is useful because no matter how smart you are... or how well you know the fundamentals behind a resource company... **you never know just how much the market will fall in love with a stock.**

The market often pushes winning resource plays to levels well beyond reason.

By setting a trailing stop, you're able to sit with your winner, instead of selling it too early and missing out on gains.

My colleague Steve Sjuggerud encourages folks to think of profit-taking situations like this: We got in early and picked a great seat in the middle of the movie theater. We've enjoyed a great show. But we think the show might be ending... and the crowd in the theater could head for the exits at any time. So we're going to move to the seat next to the exit.

We're not "leaving" just yet. We're tightening our trailing stops to preserve gains and ride the trend as long as it lasts... while staying ready to exit before a possible stampede.

So... during the incredible run we had with ATAC, we tightened our trailing stop to 25%... rode the stock a little longer... and then tightened the trailing stop again to 10%.

Ultimately, we were stopped out at $5.65 per share on September 8, 2010 for a 542% gain.

ATAC Resources (ATC.V)

www.stansberryresearch.com

The secret to our success was simple. We had an exit plan all the way.

We started with a wide stop, to account for the natural volatility in small resource stocks. As the gains came in and shares stretched higher, we tightened the stop to protect our profits. That allowed us to catch more upside without jeopardizing our gains.

In short, it allowed us to maximize our gains and minimize our risk. Let me show you another example...

CARBO Ceramics makes a special product called "proppant."

Proppant is used in the hydraulic fracturing process to "prop" open the cracks made when the company forces water down the bore hole. Hydraulic fracturing (or "fracking") is the technique that <u>blew the doors off the U.S. oil and gas industry</u>. Suddenly, we could get natural gas and oil from rocks that were considered dead just 15 years ago.

I knew this would be a huge trend... which is why we recommended CARBO. CARBO was operating at full blast. It was building new lines of production and raising its prices... The sky was the limit.

We recommended the stock when shares were trading at $60.70. We initially placed a 25% trailing stop on our position. About a year later, we were up 130%, and it was time to tighten our stop to 15%.

At its top, the stock traded for $180 per share. We were up almost 200% on the trade. But then the stock turned down. The shares dropped as low as $94. But our tighter stop got us out at $154, for a 142% gain.

If we'd held on, we would have seen two-thirds of our profits evaporate. Take a look at a chart of the company's performance over the period we owned the shares...

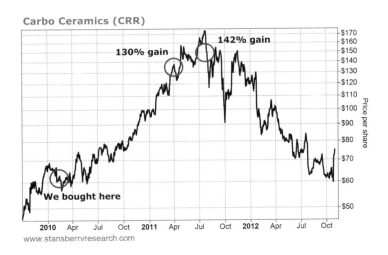

Carbo Ceramics (CRR)

www.stansberryresearch.com

Again, the secret to success was our exit plan. We didn't take profits early... and we didn't hang on too late.

These aren't isolated cases, either. Almost all of our biggest wins in the *S&A Resource Report* have played out exactly the same way. We never enter a position without an exit plan. And when a position takes off and heads hundreds of percent higher, we adjust our exit plan – we "tighten" our trailing stops to protect our gains.

Here's one more example...

In early 2009, near the depths of the credit crisis, I recommended shares of Northern Dynasty Minerals. The company owns the rights to one of the world's largest untapped gold and copper deposits. We placed a 50% trailing stop loss on the position.

Back then, the market value of Northern Dynasty was $500 million. But I thought the company was worth between $1 billion and $1.5 billion in a good market. Turns out, I underestimated our profits...

Our shares had more than doubled by November 2010, so we tightened our trailing stop from 50% to 25% to help protect our gains. But the stock continued to rip higher on news of a possible takeover, and we tightened the stop loss again to lock in this huge gain.

We sold near the top, ultimately capturing a 322% gain... and sidestepping an eventual 70% drop.

Northern Dynasty Minerals (NAK)

In the *S&A Resource Report*, we've followed this model of taking profits in other resource firms like royalty company Silver Wheaton (+345%), Chinese gold miner Jinshan Gold (+339%), and several other triple-digit winners.

21

Stocks like these can add booster rockets to your portfolio... **But you must have a system for "ringing the cash register" and taking profits**.

Have a plan to protect your initial capital when you buy, and have a plan to take profits. You'll be a much more successful resource investor if you do.

Once you master these three ideas – navigating the booms and busts of the resource sector, the tools you need to make a trade, and maximizing your returns while reducing your risk – you're ready to consider the single most important factor in natural resource investing.

With this one number in your favor, you could see decades of outsized gains...

4

The Most Important Number in Natural Resource Investment

Becoming a rich investor is all about making the numbers work.

Successful real estate investing requires making the numbers work so you receive cash flow. Successful stock investing requires making the numbers work so you receive dividends from your investment... or stand a good chance of making capital gains.

As an investor in natural resources, it's important you know there's one big number out there working for you, every day.

I call it the "China Number." And it is the most important number in all of natural resources.

The number is 9,800.

This is the amount, in U.S. dollars, of China's per-capita GDP, according to 2013 estimates in the CIA's World Factbook. (Other organizations, like the International Monetary Fund and the World Bank, have similar numbers.)

"Per-capita GDP" is the value of all the goods and services produced in a country during a given year divided by the country's population. It is one of the best yardsticks for measuring a nation's wealth.

According to the CIA's posted numbers, China's per-capita GDP in 2013 was $9,800. That makes China the world's 121st-richest country per capita.

Here's why that number is so important...

According to 2013 estimates, the United States' per-capita GDP was $52,800... more than five times China's.

Singapore, Norway, and Switzerland are all at least five times richer than China, measured by per-capita GDP. Spain, Slovenia, Greece, Lithuania, and Estonia are all more than twice as rich as China.

China's relatively low level of economic prosperity is so important to resource investors because China is the most populous country in the world. In 2014, some 1.4 billion people live there... more than 16 times the amount of people living in the countries I just mentioned *combined*.

In 2010, China surpassed Japan to become the world's second-largest economy on a total production basis. According to the *Financial Times*, that same year, China surpassed the United States to become the world's largest manufacturer by output. China is the "world's workshop."

It earned that title because it has been the world's fastest-growing major economy for several years. China grew an average of 10% per year from 2003 to 2013. This is a breakneck growth rate for a large economy.

But remember... this rapidly growing superpower with three times the population of the United States is still poor relative to the developed world. China could double its per-person wealth, and it would still be less than half as wealthy per person as the United States.

The potential here is gigantic.

For example, the number of registered automobiles in China rose 470% from 24 million in 2003 to 137 million in 2013. The first year the country had more registered cars than motorcycles was 2011.

A doubling of China's per-person wealth will mean a lot more car sales... along with more air conditioner sales... more refrigerators... more cellular phones... more televisions... more dishwashers... more everything.

And it's going to take a mountain of commodities to build it all.

It's going to take lots of iron ore to make the steel that goes into car frames.

It's going to take lots of copper to build the cooling coils in the air conditioners and refrigerators.

It's going to take lots of coal, uranium, and natural gas to fire the power plants and generate the electricity to run the factories.

It's going to take lots of oil and gasoline to transport people, materials, and products.

China's consumption is already soaring. Take coal, for example. In 1990, China accounted for 24% of the world's coal consumption. In 2010, China consumed 50% of the world's coal. The International Energy Agency (IEA) expects China will account for nearly 60% of new global coal demand up until 2018.

The story is the same with oil. In 1990, China consumed just 3% of the world's oil supply. In 2010, that jumped to 10%.

As of mid-2014, China is the world's second-largest consumer of oil. And the price of oil is up 400% since 1990.

In 1998, China's copper imports were negligible. In 2014, it can't meet demand with domestic supplies. Its imports are skyrocketing.

China's Copper Imports

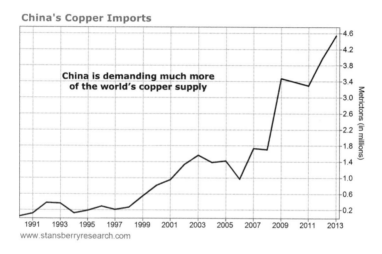

www.stansberryresearch.com

I could show you similar charts for iron ore, natural gas, coal, and many other commodities. All would show how China's consumption is booming.

Again, remember that despite all this growth, despite its position as the No. 2 economy on a total production basis, and all this natural resource consumption, China is less than one-fifth as wealthy as the United States, measured by per-person wealth.

Don't think the Chinese are happy about their low level of economic prosperity.

For 28 of the last 30 centuries, China was either the largest or the second-largest economy in the world. China has a long and proud tradition of economic progress and innovation. It invented papermaking, printing, gunpowder, and the compass.

But things took a turn in the 1800s. Brutal political struggles and a series of military defeats at the hands of Europe sent the country into chaos.

Japan took the opportunity to kick its neighbor while it was down in the late 1800s and early 1900s. It murdered and pillaged its way around China for decades. World War II brought more death and disaster... and so did a bout with crazy communist policies for much of the 20th century.

But starting around 1980, the sleeping dragon woke up. A man named Deng Xiaoping became China's leader. Deng spearheaded economic reforms and turned the busted communist ship around. He encouraged the Chinese to work hard and become rich. He freed up the economy and allowed citizens to enjoy the fruits of their labor.

What followed was one of the greatest economic booms in history.

China has gone from a land of misery and collectivism dominated by foreign powers to reassert itself as one of the most dynamic, powerful nations on earth.

And as the Chinese read, see, and hear about how wealthy industrialized nations like the U.S. and Germany have become, they work furiously to play catch up. They want the good life and the prestige that the West enjoys.

Legendary investor Jim Rogers has seen China up close... and he's always pointing out how the Chinese are more hard-working and better capitalists than U.S. citizens.

The country's rise is just beginning. China is poor compared to the rest of the world. And while it consumes awesome amounts of resources, that consumption is a fraction of what it will become...

Please keep in mind... I'm not saying, "The world is running out of resources!" I'm not worried about the world going through a huge crisis because some key resource is depleted. Prices will simply rise to reflect the supply/demand situation... and folks around the world will find substitutes for a raw material that gets very expensive.

Plus, we'll continue to find more efficient ways to use raw materials.

I'm also NOT saying China's path to economic resurgence will be smooth. There will be booms and busts along the way. The U.S. had plenty of booms and busts during its rise to power.

But the entrance of China into the modern, global economy means prices will have super-strong buying support. That's why, when periodic selloffs make resources cheap, it's a great idea to buy with both hands.

As I've said, investing in the resource sector can earn you more money than you know what to do with. But it doesn't come without its risks...

Remember... natural resources are extremely volatile. So if you are already rich, and are more interested in preserving capital than making more of it, this may not be the sector for you.

The "Chindia" Number

Another big factor that will influence commodity prices is the modernization of India.

Like China, India has more than 1 billion people. And while it has become a much more advanced nation in the past 20 years, it's still extremely poor on a per-person basis. It's less than half as wealthy as China... and less than one-tenth as wealthy as the United States.

Like China, India has a tremendous amount of "catch up" to play... and will consume an enormous amount of metals and energy in the next few decades.

But for those of you interested in investing and speculating in the resource sector, always keep in mind these three important ideas...

1. Understand the role cyclicality has on resource stocks... and how you can navigate the volatility to come out with the highest gains.

2. Study all the tools at your disposal to decide for yourself how much risk and volatility you can tolerate in your resource portfolio.

3. Set a trailing stop and stick to it.

If you stick with the strategies laid out in this guide, resource stocks have the potential to make you a millionaire.

5

A Guide to Avoiding the Most Popular Mining Scam in the World
How the unintended consequences of Bre-X could cost you a fortune

They found Michael de Guzman's body in the jungle.

It was decomposed beyond recognition.

Some people claimed he was murdered. Some claim he committed suicide because of a guilty conscience...

In the mid-1990s, de Guzman's employer was a global sensation. A geologist, de Guzman served as the exploration manager for Bre-X Minerals... a small Canadian mining company that claimed to have found a large gold deposit in Indonesia.

Actually, "large" only begins to describe the deposit de Guzman and his employers claimed to have found.

A gold deposit of 10 million ounces is considered huge by modern-day standards. *But Bre-X claimed it was sitting on over 70 million ounces of gold, with the potential for 200 million... which would have made it the largest untapped gold deposit on Earth.*

An outside company audited Bre-X's claims. It agreed that Bre-X had a stupendous find. Investors went wild. Wall Street funds bought up shares. Canadian pension plans bought up shares. Giant mining companies wrestled to get control of possibly the largest gold find in human history.

Bre-X shares climbed from C$0.45 to C$28 from June 1995 to May 1996... a gain of 6,122% in under a year.

Then, the truth came out...

On March 19, 1997, de Guzman fell to his death from a helicopter 800 feet above the jungle. His body was found four days later, decomposed and partially eaten by jungle creatures. A great unraveling of the story followed...

De Guzman had faked Bre-X's drill samples. He'd "salted" thousands of rocks with gold flakes before they were tested. The company had duped everyone.

As you can see in the chart below, shares fell from C$15.80 to C$0.08 in just 28 days. That's a 99% loss in less than a month.

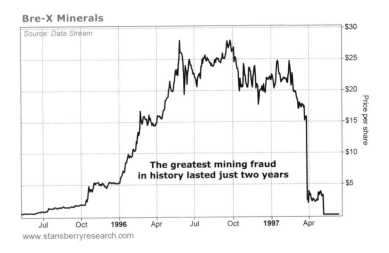

Bre-X Minerals

The greatest mining fraud in history lasted just two years

www.stansberryresearch.com

The industry considers it the greatest mining fraud in history.

If you're a longtime resource investor, you know the Bre-X story. You know it was an incredible hoax. You know about de Guzman's suspicious death.

What you may not know is that in the aftermath of Bre-X, the Canadian Securities Administrators (the Canadian equivalent to the Securities & Exchange Commission) created something called "National Instrument 43-101" (NI 43-101).

NI 43-101 is a set of rules public companies in Canada must follow when reporting information related to their mineral properties. It was intended to protect investors from mining frauds... But it has likely led to more investor losses than anything Bre-X ever did.

It is one of the most dangerous things a resource investor will encounter... ever.

What follows is a brief history of NI 43-101... how mining companies use it to dupe investors... and what you need to know to protect yourself. Revealing all this won't win me any friends in the mining industry... but it could save you a fortune.

'It's a Joke...'

"It's a joke. It's not protecting you guys in any way, shape, or form."

Joseph Conway doesn't think much of NI 43-101. He's the CEO of Primero Mining, a billion-dollar gold and silver producer. Conway has decades of high-level mining experience. In September 2013, at banking giant Scotiabank's big mining conference, he gave investors the warning above.

Over the past decade, I've talked with dozens of mining executives, insiders, and analysts. Many echo Conway's thoughts on NI 43-101. But as you can imagine, not everyone in mining wants to be on the record criticizing securities laws.

It's best to keep your head down, run your projects, and avoid rocking the boat. However, many insiders have allowed me to quote them on the condition of anonymity.

One CEO of a well-known exploration firm put it like this:

> The NI 43-101 report was thought to be the end-all, be-all of disclosure and we would never have frauds like Bre-X again. Wrong.
>
> Frauds will happen again because crooks don't play by the rules. The illusion of [NI 43-101] being a safety blanket that financial analysts could use to plug into their spreadsheets has collectively been more damaging then the out-and-out frauds.

How could such a well-intentioned idea – protecting investors – generate such criticism? How could it cost investors millions of dollars every year? How can it be more dangerous than the greatest mining scam of all time?

To get the answers, we need to cover exactly what NI 43-101 is supposed to do...

The goal of the NI 43-101 is to "ensure that misleading, erroneous, or fraudulent information... is not published and promoted on the stock exchanges overseen by the Canadian Securities Administrators."

NI 43-101 requires that mining companies publish the details of their mining projects in three different kinds of independent reports: a preliminary economic assessment (PEA), a pre-feasibility study, and a feasibility study.

Investors can find these reports on the companies' websites. Each provides the same information in increasing detail: the amount of metal in the ground ("resources"), the amount of metal that can be mined economically ("reserves"), and the economic value of the project. These reports are spaced out over the life of a project... Companies can go years between publishing them.

These documents assign a dollar amount to the mining project. Investors can – and are encouraged to – use that value to estimate how much the company is worth. On the surface, the numbers appear legitimate. The rules require that the three reports be produced and certified by independent experts.

But every year, stockbrokers, investor-relations firms, and even mining companies themselves use these reports to push up the share price. It's such a widespread practice because it's so easy to do... and so persuasive to investors.

While the NI 43-101 requirements make investors feel good, they've actually made it more dangerous for investors today than before Bre-X.

In the sections below, we're going to focus on the biggest "cheat sheets" in the mining industry... the PEA. Pre-feasibility and feasibility reports are just as likely to have flaws. But the PEA is the least-expensive report to create and requires the least detail... So it is the easiest to "fudge."

It's an open secret in the mining business that many PEAs contain exaggerations, misleading statements, and outright falsehoods.

Companies can usually find an incompetent or amoral engineer to certify the information.

As another CEO remarked:

> These documents are an average investor's worst nightmare... [The mining sector] is probably the most specialist type of investing that exists. It can gobble up generalists faster than lightning, all under the guise of "professionally certified" data!

My team and I have spent hundreds of hours on these documents over the years. What we've found made me so angry that I decided to dedicate a chapter of this book to showing you how to tell a good PEA from a bad one.

I want you to be the best-informed investor out there. I want investor-relations folks to stammer and stutter when they talk PEAs with you.

In this chapter, we'll go over all the ways that mining executives can (deliberately or not) use a PEA to dupe investors...

How NI 43-101 Fools Investors

The August 2013 issue of the *S&A Resource Report* was called, "Buying at the Bottom – Your Guide to Making Triple-Digit Returns in Cheap Gold Stocks." In it, I told readers about junior gold miner International Tower Hill Mines (ITH)...

Back in 2011, this mining company's Livengood gold project near Fairbanks, Alaska was worth an estimated $900 million. Gold had been in a bull market for 10 years. The gold price was up to $1,500 per ounce. Shares of ITH were trading for over $10 per share.

But in July 2013, ITH announced a new feasibility study on Livengood. It showed the world that the project was terrible. The results were so bad that the study couldn't make it any prettier. Investors who had purchased shares based on the PEA and previous information from management suffered large losses upon the release of the new study.

The problem was Livengood's fundamentals. It was a giant, low-grade gold deposit with a huge price tag. It was going to cost $2.8 billion to build the mine. Over the life of the mine, it would cost $1,450 per ounce to operate... That's a huge hurdle for any mine, but if the price of gold kept going up, it would be worth all the work...

According to the report, if the gold price was $2,200 per ounce, the project was worth about $2.2 billion. If the price of gold was $1,600 per ounce, the project was worthless. In July 2013, gold was around $1,300 per ounce.

At that price, the value of the project was -$1.3 billion. If we used $1,200 per ounce of gold as our price, the project was worth -$1.8 billion.

That is the kind of critical information we can glean from PEAs. The engineers who write these reports estimate all kinds of things, from the price of diesel fuel to the price of metals to the cost of construction. And they must disclose those estimates to us.

That's why one of the largest stock brokers in Canada told me that the assumptions page is far more important than the executive summary.

It's in the assumptions that most companies try to fool us.

That's where they "put the lipstick on the pigs" to make them attractive to unwary investors.

Remember, if we just assumed that the gold price was going to $2,200 per ounce, then Livengood would have been a worthwhile project. But by mid-2013, the price of gold had collapsed to around $1,200 per ounce and capital costs soared. The Livengood project was worthless.

ITH was not trying to defraud investors. It did something many mining companies have done over the years. It followed a bull market in gold and went after a bad project.

For investors, understanding the problems with assumptions is the only way to approach PEA reports. We lack the technical expertise to make informed investment decisions based on the details of the deposits. However, we can look for potentially disastrous estimates, like a gold price that's too high or a discount rate that's too low.

The next section digs into the important assumptions in these reports. It will get a little dense, but stay with me. **If you invest in mining companies on your own, this will be the some of the most valuable information you'll ever read**.

The Two Places That
Tell the Truth in Every PEA

For all three reports – PEA, pre-feasibility, and feasibility – we want to know the assumptions the company is making about the project.

1. What is the price of the metal or metals?

2. What discount rate does the company use?

3. What is the value of the project after taxes?

We'll continue to use the Livengood gold project as an example, but you can apply these guidelines to any NI 43-101 reports that contain net present value (NPV).

To find the two places that tell the truth in every PEA, go straight to the NPV calculations.

First, check the gold price. Anything over the current gold price is too high.

Next, check the "discount rate." If it's under 10%, it's too low. And make sure you're looking at values after taxes.

Here's why...

The table below comes straight out of Livengood's feasibility report from July 2013. It shows just how sensitive a big mining project can be to changes in the gold price.

Gold Price (per oz.)	Net Present Value	Change in Value
$2,200	$2.2 billion	-
$2,100	$1.9 billion	-$300 million
$2,000	$1.5 billion	-$400 million
$1,900	$1.1 billion	-$400 million
$1,800	$723 million	-$377 million
$1,700	$336 million	-$387 million
$1,600	-$50 million	-$386 million
$1,500	-$440 million	-$390 million
$1,400	-$854 million	-$414 million
$1,300	-$1.3 billion	-$446 million
$1,200	-$1.8 billion	-$500 million

Source: ITH Livengood feasibility study July 2013

As you can see, each $100-per-ounce decline in the gold price knocked $300 million-$500 million off the value of the project.

For example, if we use $2,000 per ounce for the gold price, this project appears to be worth $1.5 billion. At a market value of under $100 million, the company would appear to be an incredibly good investment...

But as we know, at $1,300 per ounce, this project – and ITH – is worthless. In December 2010, the company's shares traded for $10. By mid-2014, shares had fallen to just $0.75. That's a 93% loss. And that's exactly what we want to avoid.

How to Find the 'Right' Gold Price

The first question we should ask of every project is what would it be worth at different metal prices?

What would it be worth at $1,100 per ounce of gold?

How about $1,000 per ounce?

Goldman Sachs' analysts predicted the price of gold would fall to $1,050 per ounce in 2014. The Livengood report didn't even consider that gold price. When you know $1,200 per ounce of gold would sink the project, there isn't much reason to consider a lower gold price.

The industry usually uses a trailing three-year average gold price as a rule of thumb. That has worked out to be a great price for them, since gold spent 11 years (2002 to 2012) in a bull market roaring straight up.

But in early 2014, the trailing average was $1,542 per ounce. At the same time, the actual price of gold was around $1,300... which made the trailing three-year average price useless.

In the Livengood example, the difference between the three-year gold price and the early 2014 price was more than $1 billion in value.

How to Find the 'Right' Net Present Value

The second question to ask is how the value of the project is calculated. NPV is an estimate of the value of a project at the current time.

Some investors just assume that the NPV is equal to the numbers presented... but that's not the case. Investors must dig into the details.

Not doing so is a great way to lose a lot of money. To be successful mining investors, we have to understand how companies can manipulate the NPV.

There are three major ways for companies to cheat on that calculation: cash flows, discount rate, and gold price. We've already discussed gold price, so let's look at the other two.

A project becomes more valuable as its net cash flows (revenues minus expenditures) increase. A company can intentionally increase the value of a project by showing higher cash inflows and/or lower cash outflows than it really expects.

Of course, these are forecasts. No one really knows what will happen in the future. We've seen how small changes to the gold price can have gigantic effects on the cash flow.

There are two areas where companies can "pad" their net cash flows: capital expenditures and taxes.

Global consulting firm Accenture conducted interviews of 31 mining and metals executives in 2012. The purpose of the talks was to assess how well metals and mining companies could build projects.

A huge majority of respondents – 78% – said completing projects on time and on budget is critical to performing well.

However, only 30% of them were able to deliver projects within 25% of their budget. That means if a company expected to build a mine for $2 billion, less than a third of them got it done for under $2.5 billion. Only 17% of the executives said they were able to complete the project within 10% of budget.

We can take that to mean most of these PEAs underestimate capital expenditures.

When you are looking at forecasted capital costs on PEAs, add at least 25% to the total to be conservative. The result will be a lower project value, but it will likely be more accurate based on recent history.

Companies can also pad their values through taxes. PEAs generally present the value of a project before and after taxes. Taxes on mines vary from region to region and country to country.

A company can inflate the value of its projects by showing investors a pre-tax NPV. Make sure you find the after-tax NPV in the study.

The most common way that companies can fool us is through the "discount rate." Technically, the discount rate is the rate of return required by lenders to compensate them for the use of their money.

Think of this as the interest rates charged on mine construction loans. The higher the discount rate, the more expensive the use of the money is... and the lower the current value of a project.

The discount rate should also reflect the risk of the specific project... But it almost never does.

Mining projects are risky. The projects take too long to build, are often over budget, and last just a few years before they are mined out. That's if they are built at all. These kinds of risks would send most lenders running.

But the "official" value of most projects, certified by outside experts, is based on a discount rate suitable for a nearly risk-free lending situation.

The mining industry discount rate ranges from 0% to 10% in nearly all PEAs. It's one of those, "this is how we've always done it" rationales. And the lower the discount rate, the higher the value.

I spoke with a mining finance expert who reviews these numbers all the time. He uses a complex system to determine the appropriate project discount rates, but it's rarely under 10%. Given his impressive success rate, we want to follow his lead.

When reviewing a PEA, you should use the highest discount rate presented, or at least 10%.

This will give you a conservative estimate for the project. Some knowledgeable resource financiers use higher discount rates in their private, in-house valuation calculations. But mining companies themselves often use ridiculously low discount rates to make the projects look more valuable.

Again, we can use a real table from the Livengood PEA for an example of how a higher discount rate (one that makes more sense) drastically changes the value of a project. Notice how much the value changes even when the gold price is the same...

With gold at $1,500 per ounce, this project is worth $532 million... as long as we don't use a discount rate or consider taxes. If we use the same gold price, but a conservative discount rate of 10% and factor in taxes... this project loses $828 million!

	No Discount	5%	7.5%	10%
Pre-Tax NPV	$532 million	-$300 million	-$552 million	-$735 million
After Tax NPV	$304 million	-$440 million	-$665 million	-$828 million

The difference between an undiscounted pre-tax NPV and the after-tax, 10% discounted NPV was a staggering $1.4 billion.

As you can see, simple changes in the assumptions take this from a project worth owning to something we need to avoid at all costs.

— Part 2—

How to Make Commodity Investing Nearly Risk Free

By Porter Stansberry, founder, Stansberry & Associates

— Part 2 —

How to Make Commodity Investing Nearly Risk Free

A Case Study in Trading a Huge Resource Cycle

By Porter Stansberry, founder, Stansberry & Associates

For most people, investing in commodities is an extremely risky activity.

That's because most people are totally unaware of a way to make investing in commodities almost *risk free.*

Rather than give you a bunch of theory, I'd rather show you precisely how I put these ideas to work, starting in 2001...

At the time, I was a vehement and frequent critic of "Peak Oil."

Promoters of this idea were the most intellectually dishonest people I have ever met. The true believers were worse. They were criminally stupid. There was no way we were going to run out of oil or any other hydrocarbon, as they claimed. Not any time in the next 100 or more years.

But such arguments did scare people. They sold a lot of books. They raised a lot of money for oil companies, even for idiots who proposed *importing* natural gas into the American market. (That's like setting up a business to import oil to Saudi Arabia.)

Meanwhile, while the press and the promoters were crowing about Peak Oil and starting a panic, the actual leaders of the oil business in the United States were figuring out how to combine hydraulic fracking and horizontal drilling to produce huge amounts of gas and oil from shale rock.

One of the first was Mitchell Energy, which began producing huge volumes of gas out of the Barnett Shale (north of Dallas) in the early 2000s. Devon Energy bought the company for $3.5 billion in 2001.

Note the date. *By 2001, everyone in the oil business knew large increases to domestic onshore production were possible.* It took a while, of course, for the industry to figure out how to optimize and economize the strategies that Mitchell pioneered.

But everyone should have known – as I did – that new technology, massive increases to drilling, and rapidly growing production would eventually create a glut. The risk wasn't that we would run out of hydrocarbons. *The risk was that too much capital would be invested in the fields and that a glut would develop.*

As early as 2006, I began to warn that a huge natural-gas glut was inevitable. From the June 2006 issue of my *Investment Advisory*...

> As more rigs come on-line and consumers use less natural gas because of its high price, guess what is bound to happen? A glut of natural gas, with more and more natural gas in storage. Is that happening? Is there a glut of natural gas developing?
>
> Right now, there's 41% more natural gas in storage than average for this time of year. That's how markets work: The price of the commodity goes up, increased production follows, consumer behavior is impacted by higher prices, and, eventually, a surplus leads to lower prices.
>
> It's not about Peak Oil. It's simply a regular commodity cycle. Boom precedes bust. And when it comes to natural gas, unlike housing, we can't just sit on the extra capacity. It has to be either stored or liquidated. That's why natural gas prices might go lower than anyone expects, for a long time... Natural gas could fall even further to below $3.

Keep in mind, when I wrote that, I had no idea that the global economy would collapse in 2008. I simply knew that there was far too much capital being put to work in oil and gas fields... that prices were far too high based on inventories... and that marginal producers would continue producing for years, simply to keep cash coming in the door.

As late as 2009, I was still expecting natural gas to fall below $3 per thousand cubic feet (MCF). At a conference that March, I famously told global resource expert and longtime natural gas investor Rick Rule, "If you're long natural gas, you should have your head examined."

I then bet him a case of fine Bordeaux wine that prices would continue falling to below $3. They did. (Rick, being a man of his word, paid up.)

I want you to understand... I wasn't trying to predict the future. I simply knew that all over the U.S., formerly marginal drilling sites were being turned into gushers with new technology that was becoming more and more efficient.

44

I knew production was soaring. And I knew natural gas consumption was *falling* because high prices were leading power companies to burn more coal. Supply was soaring. Demand was falling. Inventories were bulging.

And best of all, the public was fully entranced by the nonsense of Peak Oil. There was only one possible outcome: a huge glut of natural gas. This *isn't* rocket science. It's common sense. You can see what inevitably happened below...

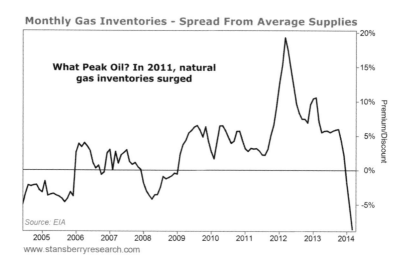

Monthly Gas Inventories - Spread From Average Supplies

What Peak Oil? In 2011, natural gas inventories surged

Source: EIA

www.stansberryresearch.com

The trick to buying commodities is to wait until there's a bust.

Wait until prices for the commodity have fallen so low that producers can't produce the commodity at a profit. Wait until inventories have surged and rolled over. Wait until prices have reached a nonsensical level. And remember... these trends take a long time to develop.

Natural Gas: Bearish to Bullish

With natural gas, I went from bearish to bullish in the spring of 2012. Here's what I wrote in my April 2012 issue, titled "The Best Opportunities of the Next Two Years"...

> I am extremely bullish on natural gas... For most investors, the opportunity unfolding in natural gas will be one of the best investment opportunities of the next decade.
>
> Right now, natural gas is so cheap that many companies are simply flaring it off – they're burning it – rather than bothering to

pipe it across the country and sell it. Not only that, but right now, you can buy natural gas reserves in the stock market for *free*.

Sooner or later, the price of natural gas will rebound sharply... and not just because it always has in the past. What will propel natural gas prices over the medium term (say, five years) is an economic truism: It's impossible for a surplus of *energy* to exist for long.

As prices fall, more and more uses for natural gas will appear. At some price, natural gas becomes competitive with other forms of energy. *In my mind, you ought to buy all the natural gas you can afford because these energy resources will not be cheap forever.*

By the spring of 2012, I knew a few things that gave me total confidence that natural gas prices had reached a bottom...

First, I knew that with the spot price under $2 per MCF, it was impossible for any of the independent natural-gas companies (Devon, Chesapeake, Anadarko, Southwestern, Encana, WPX, and Ultra) to make money.

The chart below shows how their operating margins were collapsing as their hedges rolled off and they began transacting at the new, much lower price of gas...

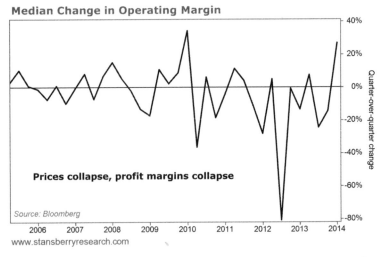

Median Change in Operating Margin

Prices collapse, profit margins collapse

Source: Bloomberg

www.stansberryresearch.com

Second, because natural gas is only one form of hydrocarbon energy, I could see that it had reached a comparative price that was simply unthinkable. The real commodity you're buying when you buy natural gas is *energy*. At some price, all forms of hydrocarbons are relatively interchangeable.

46

For decades, oil has been about 10 times more expensive than natural gas, on average, on an energy-equivalent basis. But by the spring of 2012, oil was trading for more than 50 times the price of natural gas. There was no way that such a price disparity would last because one form of energy is ultimately interchangeable with another...

Oil-to-Natural-Gas Ratio

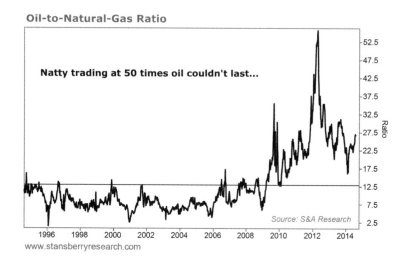

By the spring of 2012, we could see that a glut had developed (as we had expected). We could see that prices had collapsed to *historic lows*. We could see that the marginal producers (the U.S. independents) were going to experience massive operating losses.

But how did we know the time was truly right? Our timing was dictated by significant reductions to both production and inventories.

The next chart shows the natural-gas-rig count maintained by oil-services giant Baker Hughes. It's the number of rigs that were working in the U.S. to produce natural gas from 2004 to mid-2014. You can see that in 2012, the rig count plummeted. That's the producers "taking their ball and going home"...

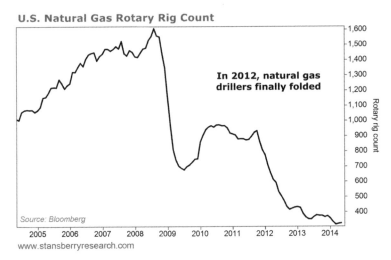

U.S. Natural Gas Rotary Rig Count

In 2012, natural gas drillers finally folded

Source: Bloomberg

www.stansberryresearch.com

This move – plus a large and surprising decline in natural-gas inventories in March 2012 – was the final sign I had been waiting to see. The neat thing about commodity markets is that they are purely logical. High prices (during a boom) spur production and cause consumers to reduce consumption.

But at the bottom, the opposite occurs. After gas prices crashed, we saw all kinds of new demand for natural gas emerge because the price was so low. We saw a surge in exports. We saw power companies switch from coal back to natural gas. And we saw global manufacturing relocate to the U.S. to take advantage of the surplus of cheap energy – particularly the petrochemical industry.

Reduce Your Risk by 90% in Commodities

If you go back and look at the best-performing S&P 500 companies over the long term, you'll find that many of them are energy companies. That's because the operating margins and returns on investment in the resource sector (particularly energy) can be huge. Investing in commodity stocks is generally perceived as risky.

But using a small amount of common sense and information that's widely available to all investors... it's not only possible, it's *easy* to identify safe opportunities to invest in commodities.

The trick is waiting until prices are so low, the entire production industry is failing... and then not 'pulling the trigger' until inventories begin to sharply decline. Also remember that these cycles are long-lived.

You might only get the kind of opportunity we saw in natural gas back in 2012 once or twice every 20 years. You have to watch these markets over the long term and be prepared to make large commitments when the time is right.

There are two more things you should know about investing in commodities... two genuine "inside" secrets that few people will ever explain to you. *If you watch the cycle develop like I describe, you can reduce your risk by 90%.*

All you have to be is patient. You can't force a commodity-price cycle to change. **If you're able to be patient, you can virtually eliminate the remaining risk by only investing in royalty-paying securities**. These are companies – like natural gas royalty trust San Juan Royalty Trust (SJT) – that simply own royalty interests in wells or mines.

The cool thing about these trusts is that their payout increases tend to follow commodity-price changes by about six months. If you look at San Juan Royalty Trust, for example, it really began to move higher in 2013, even though natural-gas prices bottomed in April 2012.

We call this **the "royal" delay**. It gives investors a second chance to buy into the bottom of a commodity. That's great for obvious reasons, but *the real reason royalty trusts help you eliminate investment risk is because they don't have any debt or any overhead*. It's next to impossible for them to go bankrupt.

The "Royal" Delay

Royalty stocks often trail commodity prices by six to 12 months, offering investors a "second chance" to invest at the bottom... (5-year chart)

www.stansberryresearch.com

49

The other, safer, option than buying the producers is to focus on the "picks and shovels" companies. Take Halliburton, for example. It's one of the leading providers of services to the production companies I listed. Its shares climbed 150% from mid-2012 to mid-2014! That's a far better return than almost all other producers.

The great thing about buying a well-run services company is that you get industry-wide diversification. All production companies use Halliburton's services. Thus, you don't have to try to figure out which fields are the best or which producer is going to strike the biggest wells.

Whoever is doing best will be using Halliburton. You can accomplish much the same by buying low-risk ETFs that hold stakes in all of the producers, like FRAK, for example.

The point is... investing in the commodity-price cycle can be low risk if you buy securities like royalty trusts, service companies, or ETFs that don't have any single-stock risk.

If you combine this approach with buying a few of the highest-quality producers (think EOG in the Eagle Ford Shale, Devon in the Permian Basin, or Continental in the Bakken Shale), you'll be successful.

Most investors think investing in commodity businesses is risky. *But if you're willing to time the commodity-price cycle and if you focus on royalty firms and "picks and shovels" plays, these investments can be among the safest you'll ever make.*

In the right circumstances, you can produce trades with zero downside risk and huge upside potential. Just remember to wait for **historically low prices, collapsing profit margins (in the producers)**, and **suddenly shrinking inventories**.

— Part 3—

Useful Interviews for Natural Resource Investors

— Part 3 —

The World's Greatest Investment Ideas

Interview Series

Over the years, Stansberry & Associates has produced a large educational interview series called "The World's Greatest Investment Ideas."

In this series, S&A analysts and contacts discuss the world's most useful wealth and investment ideas. It covers how to succeed in real estate... how to identify a great business... the best way to invest in agriculture... and the best type of stock to own to collect investment income.

A handful of these "World's Greatest Investment Ideas" interviews focus on natural resources.

In Part II of *Secrets of the Natural Resource Market*, you'll find some of the most useful ideas for making money in natural resources.

Resources legend Rick Rule discusses what could be the simplest way to invest in commodities. Gold-stock expert John Doody describes an incredible business model for profiting in gold mining.

Editor of S&A's *True Wealth* advisory Steve Sjuggerud reveals one of his favorite natural resource investments. And S&A Editor in Chief Brian Hunt talks about a "sleep at night" way to make huge returns in booming commodities sectors.

If you're looking to make life-changing profits from the natural resource sector, read on...

Resource 'Hoarding'

February 19, 2012

In this interview, master resource investor Rick Rule discusses one of the most powerful strategies for profiting in natural resources...

Rick has spent decades in the resource markets, making himself and his clients a fortune in the process. He has also financed several of the most important resource companies in the world. No one is more qualified to explain this idea.

What you'll read below is not complicated, but don't let that fool you. Rick has personally used this idea to make mind-boggling amounts of money in resource stocks.

If you're looking to do the same, read on...

———————————•———————————

Stansberry & Associates: Rick, of all the ways to invest in resources, the strategy of "hoarding" may be the simplest... But it can also be extremely profitable – and relatively safe – when done correctly. Before we get into how this idea works, can you define what hoarding is?

Rick Rule: Sure. Hoarding is simply buying resources in the ground and holding them, rather than mining or extracting them. Companies that do this are known as "hoarders."

S&A: What is the benefit of hoarding?

Rule: To fully appreciate the beauty of the strategy, you must first understand a fact about the mining business: It's a *terrible* business.

It's a business where your asset base – the resources in the mine – is declining consistently over time, you have huge capital costs for building the mines and maintaining expensive equipment, and you're often exposed to huge political risks because you can't just pack up a mine and move it. On top of all that, many mining executives are less than shareholder-friendly.

So when you buy a mining stock, you must understand that is the business you're buying into.

Now imagine if you could get many of the positives of owning the resources in a mine, but without the negatives associated with mining. That is the benefit of hoarding.

Hoarders accumulate mines and undeveloped resource deposits, and basically just sit on them. Because they don't operate mines, they don't have the huge capital costs and risks of traditional mining companies.

Their share price is simply a leveraged play on the price of the underlying resource. When prices rise, the value of the company's deposits increase as well.

S&A: You've been intimately involved with this strategy... Can you give us some examples of how profitable it can be?

Rule: Certainly. During the bear market in resources during the 1990s and early 2000s, we were able to employ this strategy with great success.

At the time, there was no constituency for resource stocks at all. A group of us in the business came to the realization that exploring for things like heavy oil, natural gas, copper, uranium, and even gold and silver made no sense at the time.

But we could buy the successful efforts of prior explorers – where the deposits weren't profitable at the then-prevailing prices – often for pennies on the dollar. Because we believed that commodity prices had nowhere to go but up, this made perfect sense.

As an example, during that time we financed Silver Standard – one of the world's biggest owners of silver mines – at $0.72 a share, or about $2 million. But instead of mining the deposits, we just held them. As other proven mines became available, we bought them, too. When silver soared in the bull market of the 2000s, it became a $1 billion-plus company.

Another great example was Paladin Resources, a uranium hoarder. It was buying uranium when absolutely nobody cared about it. We bought it at $0.10 a share, and I remember selling some of that stock at $10 a share.

As you can see, the leverage these companies can provide to rising commodity prices is just incredible.

S&A: What are the guidelines for hoarding stocks?

Rule: The ideal time to buy these stocks is at the bottom of a resource cycle or during times of great pessimism. When the price of a particular commodity is low, mining companies in the sector can't produce a profit, and most investors are completely uninterested.

It's at these times when the hoarder stocks are at their cheapest, safest, and most attractive. Take uranium after the Fukushima disaster as a great example.

Of course, because hoarders are so leveraged to the price of the underlying resource, they can be a good speculation on rising prices and a hedge against inflation. Just remember that leverage is a double-edged sword, so the volatility will typically be much greater than that of the actual commodity.

I should also mention that successfully owning these stocks requires a great deal of discipline and patience. These stocks can return hundreds and hundreds of times your money, but they often require several years to do so.

Are you prepared to wait five, 10, or more years for those kinds of returns?

Most investors would impulsively say yes, but in practice, many have trouble holding a stock for 10 weeks, never mind 10 years. People want immediate gratification. But in my experience, immediate gratification is very seldom on offer in the financial markets.

S&A: That's a great point... Are there any significant risks to owning these stocks?

Rule: Because they aren't involved in the mining business, these stocks are generally less risky than the miners... But there are still some risks.

While they don't have to pay the huge capital costs of mining, they do still have to pay for expenses like property taxes, fees, and overhead. They don't mine, so they're typically cash flow negative. This means they can get into trouble and be extraordinarily volatile during times when access to capital becomes difficult. You must be prepared for that.

Also, because these companies' resource estimates are usually based on drilling and assays rather than actual production, the stocks trade at a significant discount to active mining companies. This isn't necessarily a risk, but it's another good reason to concentrate your purchases at times of great pessimism.

As I frequently say, you have to be a contrarian or you will be a victim.

S&A: Thanks for the insight, Rick.

Rule: My pleasure. Thanks for having me.

— 2 —

Mastering the Resource Market's Cyclicality

November 6, 2011

If you plan to invest one dime in natural resources like gold, oil, and uranium, this interview is a must-read.

We sat down with legendary resource investor Rick Rule to discuss how one can master the giant cycles in natural resources. Catch one of these big cycles early, and you may never have to work again. Catch one at the wrong time, and you'll lose a fortune...

If you're looking to make life-changing profits from commodities or resource stocks, read on...

———————————●———————————

Stansberry & Associates: Rick, most readers are aware of how profitable investing in commodities and natural resource stocks can be. The gains on individual positions can run into the thousands, even tens of thousands of percent.

But many people are unaware of the cyclical nature of resources... and how to use this aspect to efficiently invest or speculate in them. Could you explain how a resource cycle works?

Rick Rule: Sure. Resource markets are cyclical for two primary reasons... They are extremely capital intensive, and they are extremely time intensive. In other words, resources tend to take a great deal of time and money to produce, mine, or extract.

So when supply and demand imbalances occur, the resource sector isn't able to react as quickly as other markets. This long lag time creates huge price swings... extreme highs and extreme lows you don't see in most other markets.

When demand exceeds supply in most markets, you see a relatively quick reaction from producers to meet the new demand. Compare this to resources like copper or gold...

Before you can produce it, you have to go find it and build a mine. The exploration cycle – the pre-development cycle – can take up to 10 years. In the meantime, prices can soar, while the market waits for that increased supply.

On the other side, after supplies come onto the market, prices peak and start to fall. What happens is that the industry comes to regard their sunk costs as just that... sunk costs. So they're hesitant to slow production, in spite of high supplies and falling prices. They'll continue to produce even when prices fall below the level at which they would be profitable.

In fact, they'll often produce even below the marginal cost of production for a while in a contest known in the resource industry as "the last man standing."

The reasoning here is that it might cost them more to shut down a project and restart it than it would to continue operating at a loss. And each producer wants to be the first in the game when the cycle turns back around. This drives prices even lower than they otherwise would go.

So you have this extraordinary cyclicality as a consequence of the capital- and time-intensive nature of the business.

S&A: Can you give us a couple examples of resource cycles in action?

Rule: Sure... To give your readers a feel for the extremes of commodity cycles, let's look at uranium.

In the 1970s, uranium prices kept pace with other energy sources, escalating 10-fold. And uranium-stock share prices exceeded those commodity price escalations.

But the decline in energy prices that accompanied the worldwide economic slowdown in the early 1980s – along with the "Three Mile Island" mishap – delivered a staggering blow to uranium markets. Then the Chernobyl disaster finished them off.

The uranium bear market – beginning in 1992 and ending in 2002 – saw the uranium price decline from $35 per pound to $7 per pound. At the bottom of the market, the industry was selling the stuff for $7-$9 per pound and producing it for $18 per pound. They were losing $10 per pound and trying to make it up on volume!

Worldwide, however, we were producing 90 million pounds and consuming 150 million pounds, with the consumed surplus coming from prior excess utility inventories and conversion of weapons-grade stocks. So the price had to rebound, and it did.

In the period from 2002 to 2006, the spot price soared from $7 to $130 per pound. Meanwhile, production costs approximately doubled to $40 per pound. Since then, the price of uranium has continued to fluctuate dramatically.

The reaction of investors to these cycles is amusing, if tragic.

At the periodic highs, investors were crowding frantically into uranium equities, although the stage was set – through price-induced increases in supply and reductions in demand – for a price collapse. And of course, investors sold in disgust at market lows, when inverse conditions argued for dramatic increases in the uranium price.

S&A: Are there any tricks for distinguishing where we are in a particular commodity's cycle?

Rule: Yes... In any resource, when the industry's median production cost exceeds the commodity's selling price – in other words, when it costs companies more to produce that commodity than the commodity is worth on the market – that industry is in liquidation. This is the situation I just mentioned in uranium.

There are two potential outcomes at that point... either the price has to rise, or that commodity will no longer be for sale on the market. That is a strong sign that you're approaching or have arrived at the bottom of a cycle.

Conversely, when commodity producers as a whole enjoy 50% or better pre-tax margins and returns on capital employed exceed the S&P 500's returns on employed capital by 50% or more, you should be looking for the exits. The stage is set for a serious decline in the price on that commodity.

In other words, markets work. The cure for low prices is low prices, and the cure for high prices is high prices.

S&A: You've made a career of profiting from resource cyclicality. What advice do you have for readers to do the same?

Rule: Well, technically it's as simple as following the old Wall Street adage of "buy low and sell high." You want to buy when supply exceeds demand and prices are low, and sell when demand exceeds supply and prices are high. It sounds easy. But in practice, it's very difficult to follow.

Most people don't have the courage to buy something that is dirt-cheap and has gone nowhere for years... But that's what it takes to "buy low" in the resource sector. Similarly, most people don't have the discipline to sell something that has soared hundreds or thousands of percent... But that's what it takes to "sell high."

So the first thing that one must do is learn to master him or herself before attempting to master cyclicality.

Warren Buffett famously said you shouldn't buy a share of stock unless you know it well enough that you would be delighted to see it fall 25% in price, so you could buy more at a 25% discount.

That is also how you must approach the resource sector. Even when you buy low, it is certain many of your investments will go lower before they go higher. You absolutely will buy shares of XYZ exploration for $1 a share and see it fall to $0.70 a share. If you did your research, the stock will be a substantially better buy at $0.70 a share than it was at $1 a share, and you need to buy it.

When you buy resources stocks, you need to recognize that they're not merely trading vehicles. They represent fractional ownership of a business.

And to profit from them, you have to go through the type of analysis your colleague Dan Ferris goes through.

What's the company worth? If the company is worth $1 billion and there are 10 million shares outstanding, what is the value per share of the business?

That's a simple example, but many people don't go even that far.

If you have a good sense of what something is worth, and it declines in price... you may have the courage and the sense to buy more. If it escalates fairly rapidly in price to the point where its price exceeds your estimate of its value, you might make a rational sell decision.

But without that sort of grounding in value and understanding, most people have no business in resource stocks.

S&A: Thanks for the insight, Rick.

Rule: You're welcome. Thanks for having me.

Summary: To profit from resource cyclicality, you want to buy when supply exceeds demand and prices are low, and sell when demand exceeds supply and prices are high. Since resource stocks represent fractional ownership of a business, you must determine what the company is worth before buying the shares.

3

How to Make the Biggest, Safest Returns Possible in Royalty Companies

January 22, 2012

The interview below features one of the best precious-metals investments in the world: royalty companies.

To explain the incredible benefits of these stocks, we sat down with John Doody, one of the world's top experts on gold and silver stocks.

Whether you're just getting started in resource-stock investing or you already own some of these companies, John's advice could be critical to making the biggest, safest returns possible in this volatile sector.

———————————●———————————

Stansberry & Associates: John, you're one of the world's top experts on gold and silver stocks. And you follow several "royalty companies." Before we get into the value of owning these stocks, can you define what a royalty company is?

John Doody: A royalty company is basically a mine-financing entity that has sold shares to the public. These companies provide money to miners for either exploration or actual capital costs such as mine and processing-plant construction. So in a sense, they compete with bank lenders and equity offerings that brokers want to do for mining companies.

Royalty companies provide this financing to mining companies in exchange for one of two types of future payments.

In the first type, the royalty company will finance an exploration program to receive a royalty on any future sales that are produced from any discovery – which is kind of like a sales tax – that typically ranges from

1% to 5% of sales. While the upfront money can be small – often just a few million dollars – the royalties can be big.

One royalty company we like steadily receives about $50 million per year from a site it helped fund exploration for in the mid-1980s.

In the second type, the royalty company will help finance mine construction – which is much more expensive than funding an exploration program – and receive a royalty payment called a "stream." A stream is a commitment for either a certain number of ounces of metals per year or a certain percentage of ounces produced on an annual basis from the mine.

In this second type, a royalty company might be able to buy streams of gold at a 75% discount to the current spot price. But in order to buy gold at that kind of discount, it has to put up a significant amount of capital upfront.

Streams are often the preferred financing methods for the mining companies. If they borrow the money from a bank, they might have to hedge the production... or the bank might want more security of other mining assets, and so forth.

If they sell more shares to finance the mine, it dilutes – and irritates – existing stockholders. So it's generally an easier financing mechanism for the miners, and it's a stream of income that the royalty company earns over the life of the mine.

S&A: What makes royalty companies such great investments?

Doody: First, it's a great way to get diversification.

From an investor's standpoint, the typical mature royalty company has a portfolio of anywhere from 10 or 15 up to 50 different mines that are paying it royalties and streams.

So it's a broad, diversified portfolio compared to a typical mining company that might own one or two mines.

And as you know, there's a lot of risk associated with a one- or two-mine company. It's common to see mines encounter difficulties for various reasons, and the related mining stocks might lose 25%, 50%, or more of their value in one day.

On the other hand, if a big royalty company had a royalty on that mine, it wouldn't be a big deal, because there would be royalties from other mines that could take up the slack.

You also have a degree of transparency and clarity you don't get with mining stocks. Royalty pipelines are typically visible, particularly over a three- or four-year time frame. And once a royalty company has put the money in, it doesn't have any further risk.

If there are capital cost overruns – and that can be a big problem for mines because they often cost more to build than what was planned for – they're not the royalty company's problem. It's already struck its deal. It might take another bite of it, but that would be a new deal. It's not something that it would have to pay any portion of. The miner is responsible for all overruns in the construction budget.

There's also no exposure to the rising costs of production that miners have.

The production cost of an ounce of gold or silver has gone up dramatically over time. For example, the average cost of production for an ounce of gold in the early 2000s was around $200 an ounce. By 2012, the average cost to produce an ounce of gold was close to $650.

A third benefit of royalty companies is they typically pay higher dividends than even some of the biggest mining companies. They have very low overhead.

I don't think any of the big ones have more than 20 employees, because you don't need a lot of people in the business. And that means that a very high percentage of royalty income – typically more than 90% – goes to gross profits. From this, they pay dividends and taxes and finance future royalties and streams.

Usually, they pay out about 20% of their royalty income as a dividend, which gives you great current income and visible growth from the royalty pipeline.

S&A: Based on those traits – diversification, relative safety, and high dividends – some folks might assume these stocks don't experience big growth. Is that true?

Doody: No, not really. Royalty companies typically provide strong, steady growth... and much less risky growth, in my opinion.

One of the disadvantages of these companies is there's a lot of unfamiliarity about them among investors. They don't really understand the unique features that make them much more predictable in terms of their growth and their dividends. I think as their pluses get more widely known, their stock prices will react higher.

S&A: Can you provide a couple examples of how royalty companies can grow to the sky?

Doody: One of the best-known royalty companies is Royal Gold. It's a great example of a royalty company that started small and steadily grew to a multibillion-dollar business.

Royal Gold had the original idea of exploring to grow its own properties, and then finding majors to develop them, while retaining a royalty interest in them.

The company had explored and found gold on a property in Nevada called Cortez. It got a miner called Placer Dome to develop it, and Royal Gold kept a royalty on it. It was a much smaller property when Placer first got involved, and it turned into a million-ounce-a-year mine. That huge royalty basically funded Royal Gold's growth in the acquisition of more properties, and it snowballed from there.

S&A: Do you have any rough guidelines for buying these royalty companies?

Doody: The most important thing to know is that the big ones trade in the market at different multiples than the smaller ones. The big companies tend to trade around 20 times royalties per share.

So if a company has $2 in royalty income per share, the price would tend to average around 20 times that, or $40. Of course, that doesn't mean it can't trade between 15 and 30 times royalty income. Stocks go up and down over the course of the year. But the multiples center around 20.

The smaller companies trade at about half that. In a sense, the public market won't pay the same premium for the small royalty producers that it does for the big ones. And that's probably because there's more risk associated with the smaller ones. They have fewer royalties, so they're more exposed to mine risks. And they don't get to see a lot of big deals, so they tend to get the scraps that the big guys aren't interested in.

Ideally, you want to buy the big ones when they're trading around 15 times royalty income and sell them when they're trading over 25 times income. You want to buy the small ones when they're trading around five times royalty income and sell them when they're trading over 10 times income. But rather than trading in and out based on the multiple, it can be better to just buy and hold based on their pipeline of growth.

S&A: Any parting thoughts on royalty companies?

Doody: I'll just add that it's common for several of the 10 recommendations in our current "Top 10" portfolio to be royalty companies. That should tell you something about how much we like these stocks.

S&A: Thanks for talking with us, John.

Doody: You're welcome. Thanks for inviting me.

4

The Ultimate Agriculture Investment

May 1, 2011

This idea comes from Dr. Steve Sjuggerud, editor of *True Wealth*. The letter is published by Stansberry & Associates. It's one of the world's most popular investment advisories.

In this interview, Steve reveals one of his all-time favorite natural resource investments... an asset the average investor has never considered... but that has consistently beaten stocks and bonds for decades.

If you're like most investors, you're looking for ways to earn big, safe long-term returns. This interview will show you a great way to do so... while diversifying your money outside of the U.S. dollar and traditional investments.

———————●———————

Stansberry & Associates: You've done a tremendous amount of research on timberland investing over the years... and you've been a big proponent of this idea. You've called it "the ultimate agriculture investment." What is so special about timberland?

Steve Sjuggerud: Yes... I've been all over the world researching timberland investing. I've spent hundreds of hours on it. I've recommended many timber stocks to my readers over the years. And I've personally invested in timberland.

There's a long list of reasons why investing in timberland is a great idea... and consistently produces big returns.

First of all, trees grow year in and year out. Trees in good growing regions in the U.S. grow at 6%-8% per year. They grow through recessions. They grow through wars. They grow through stock and real estate crashes. They grow through everything. They give you built-in investment growth that isn't guaranteed with a stock.

Along with the tree growth, the price of wood has grown at a consistent rate throughout the years. It's extremely difficult for a company to increase the prices of its goods by 6% every year. But the price of wood, according to legendary money manager Jeremy Grantham, has increased by that amount for the last 100 years.

Specifically, he says "stumpage" prices – the value of all the wood on the stump – have beaten inflation by 3% a year over the last century.

Another thing is timberland is a resource investment, but it's not a constantly depleting one, like a gold mine or an oil well. Trees will grow back. It's a sustainable resource investment.

And not to ramble on, but you should know, timber is uncorrelated to the stock market. It makes sense... the trees have never heard of the Nasdaq bubble... and they don't know what a "War on Terror" is. This makes timber a great place to park money in big portfolios... where you need diversification.

S&A: But what happens to your timberland investment in a down year, when lumber prices crash?

Sjuggerud: That's a great question. What happens when the market is slumping? When you can't get the price you need to make the business profitable? Did you just waste eight... 15... 25 years on an investment with nothing to show for it? The answer can be summed up in five words: *"Bank it on the stump."*

In the industry, it's a phrase that means if conditions aren't right for harvesting your crop, you just keep letting it grow. You keep the profits on the stump and wait for a more profitable time to sell your timber – most likely, when timber prices are in your favor.

One of the great benefits of owning timberland is you don't have to harvest it every year. It's not like fruit, where it's ripe just once and then you have to pick it. Instead, it grows exponentially on the stump for years.

This is not to imply that timber is an absolutely risk-free investment... But with the ability to bank it on the stump, investing in timber does come with an extra safety net. "If the rain rains, the sun shines, the suckers grow," Jeremy Grantham once said. "If you don't want to sell, they get bigger and more expensive."

S&A: Those are tremendous attributes. How has timberland performed over the years?

Sjuggerud: Take a look at this table of the period from 1971 to 2010... which was filled with all sorts of bull and bear markets for stocks...

Year	Annual Return	Account Size
1971	4.4%	$10,000
1972	11.0%	$11,104
1973	58.7%	$17,625
1974	20.8%	$21,290
1975	1.3%	$21,564
1976	16.0%	$25,021
1977	48.5%	$37,154
1978	29.5%	$48,103
1979	31.0%	$62,991
1980	5.4%	$66,405
1981	2.6%	$68,132
1982	-1.8%	$66,919
1983	0.6%	$67,294
1984	3.2%	$69,434
1985	-2.6%	$67,656
1986	3.3%	$69,916
1987	26.6%	$88,513
1988	30.1%	$115,174
1989	37.4%	$158,191
1990	11.1%	$175,687
1991	20.3%	$211,281
1992	37.3%	$290,131
1993	22.4%	$355,033
1994	15.4%	$409,850
1995	13.8%	$466,574
1996	10.7%	$516,637
1997	18.9%	$614,333
1998	9.0%	$669,746
1999	12.9%	$756,344
2000	4.4%	$789,681
2001	-5.2%	$748,256
2002	1.9%	$762,340
2003	7.7%	$820,773
2004	11.2%	$912,697
2005	19.3%	$1,089,288
2006	13.7%	$1,238,287
2007	18.4%	$1,466,549
2008	9.5%	$1,606,184
2009	-4.8%	$1,529,730
2010	-0.2%	$1,527,309

From 1971 to 2010, an investor in timber saw average annual returns of over 14% – turning $10,000 into over $1.5 million. That's better than stocks and bonds over the same period.

Here are the rough numbers on where timberland returns come from:

- 1% Land-value increase
- 6% Biologic growth of the trees
- 3% "Stumpage" price increase (the price of the actual tree)

S&A: So timberland can serve as a good alternative investment when stocks are in a bear market?

Sjuggerud: Absolutely. One of the worst-ever bear markets in stocks began in the late 1960s and lasted until about 1980. An investor in stocks during that time lost money, due to inflation.

However, as the table shows, an investor in timber never had a losing year during that period. More often than not, the returns were in the double digits... with a 59% return in 1973 and a 49% return in 1977.

To sum up, timberland offers high returns... It is a sustainable asset that can provide returns for centuries... It has no correlation to the stock market... It's less volatile... And it constantly grows in value.

S&A: So how do you go about buying timberland? What's the easiest way to own it?

Sjuggerud: It's important to point out that rather than just going out and buying a forest, you want to make sure to invest in *managed timberland.*

The reason it's important to make the distinction is simple: Managed timberlands, according to a study conducted by the University of Georgia and published in the *Journal of Forestry*, generate returns almost four times higher than non-managed lands.

With managed timberlands, you get just what it says. You get professional managers who cultivate the trees, look after them, and harvest the trees and their products at the right time.

They look to earn extra cash by selling hunting rights to the land. They harvest and sell the straw and seeds that fall from the trees. Good managers even look to sell chunks of your timberland if a real estate developer comes along and offers a sky-high premium for your land.

My point is everything on the "tree farm" – even the tree farm itself – is for sale. You can make these types of managed timberland investments privately, or there are usually a handful of publicly traded timberland companies on the exchange at any given time.

The big names in the U.S. are Weyerhaeuser (WY), Rayonier (RYN), and Plum Creek (PCL). To spread your risk, you can buy the U.S. big names through an exchange-traded fund with the symbol: WOOD. You can get much broader international exposure through the Guggenheim Timber Fund (CUT).

S&A: There are many good points to timberland investing. Any negative ones?

Sjuggerud: When you compare the built-in yield of timberland to any other asset class out there, timberland wins hands-down.

The only problem is *time frame* – you can sell a stock or bond immediately, but you can't get rid of acres of timber like that. It's illiquid. You've got to hold it for some time to maximize its value – the ideal timeframe is infinity. It's definitely not for traders... it's for long-term thinking investors.

And keep in mind... like all investments, you have to make sure you buy timberland at a reasonable price.

S&A: Thanks, Steve.

Sjuggerud: You're welcome

— 5 —

Picks and Shovels

April 3, 2011

As Editor in Chief of Stansberry & Associates, Brian Hunt sees more investment ideas come across his desk in one week than most people do in five years.

As you'll see below, one of his top ways to make huge returns in booming sectors or commodities is "picks and shovels"... a "sleep at night" way to profit from a bull market.

———————●———————

Stansberry & Associates: For many investors, the safe, "sleep at night" way to make huge returns in booming sectors or commodities is to own the "picks and shovels" of the boom.

Can you explain how this idea works?

Brian Hunt: Sure. The idea of owning "picks and shovels" in order to profit from a big sector or commodity boom simply means owning companies that supply the vital tools, products, or services many participants in the boom must use... rather than taking the riskier route and buying the individual players in the boom.

The classic success story here was back in the 1850s, when a German immigrant moved from New York to San Francisco to participate in the California Gold Rush.

Rather than taking the "all or nothing" route of looking for a big gold strike, the German immigrant sold basic goods to the miners.

This was a much safer, surer way to acquire wealth than trying to find the one big strike.

The immigrant eventually started producing a new type of durable pants to sell to the miners. They became a huge hit... and the German immigrant got rich. His name was Levi Strauss.

Levi didn't risk it all on trying to find the big strike, he just sold the stuff everyone else needed to try to find the next big strike themselves.

S&A: How about a few modern examples?

Hunt: Two great "picks and shovels" stories of modern times come from the recent Internet and energy booms: Cisco and Core Laboratories.

Cisco was one of the ultimate "picks and shovels" investment plays of the Internet revolution.

Rather than try to pick which website companies were going to be successful, an investor could have just bought Cisco instead.

Cisco made the routers and switches – what some folks called the "plumbing" – required to build the Internet... and the stock climbed more than 9,500% from its IPO in 1992 to the 2000 bubble peak.

Remember... during this time, thousands of companies tried to become the Internet's "next big thing." A handful made it. Most did not. Cisco just sold the "picks and shovels" to build the Internet and soared. It was the surer bet. It was the "sleep at night" bet.

Now, let's take the story of Core Laboratories.

Back in 2003, if investors believed that crude oil was set for a big price rise, they had a handful of different vehicles to choose from.

They could buy speculative futures contracts... they could buy a small oil company exploring for oil in some remote jungle... or they could have bought shares in Core Laboratories.

Core Laboratories used specialized technology to analyze oil and gas deposits. They helped oil companies decide where to drill in order to find big deposits and helped them manage those deposits once they were found.

Core did no drilling or exploration of its own. It was paid by lots of different market participants who were doing lots of drilling and exploration.

As oil prices climbed from $30 per barrel in 2003 to $100 per barrel in 2008, Core's customers had more money to spend on exploration. Core's revenues surged... and the stock went from $5 per share to $60 per share... a gain of 1,100%.

It was a pure "picks and shovels" play on the oil boom. Rather than take on the risk of owning shares in a company looking for oil in just a handful of places, Core Laboratories investors could sleep soundly. They knew the company was collecting a steady stream on money from a huge number of oil companies.

S&A: Most people don't realize there are "picks and shovels" investments in nearly every industry.

Can you give us a few more examples most folks don't realize exist?

Hunt: Sure. I have two more. Let's talk farming, then biotechnology.

In 2006, corn and soybean prices entered a big bull move that took both crops more than 200% higher.

Emerging markets like China started growing richer and consuming more livestock... which resulted in increased demand for grain to feed the livestock.

Rather than going out and buying a farm... or going into the futures market to buy corn and soybeans, an investor could have bought shares in fertilizer producers like Potash and Mosaic. These two companies produce and sell the vital fertilizers farmers slather on their fields to increase crop yields.

As crop prices climbed and farm incomes rose, demand for fertilizers increased. Potash shares gained 600% during the boom... Mosaic gained 900%.

Again, we see huge returns were made in companies that sold vital tools, products, and services used by an industry in a big upswing.

Now, developing drugs in the biotechnology field is a lot different from farming, but it has its "picks and shovels" plays as well. For example, there's a type of business called contract research organizations, or CROs.

These are companies that perform lab and testing work for big pharmaceutical and small drug-development companies. They assist these companies with the huge undertaking of developing and testing new drugs they hope to one day sell for billions of dollars.

Many drug companies are risky bets on just one or two drugs making it to market. CROs aren't like that. They just do research and development. When the industry is in an upswing, CROs take in revenue from lots of different clients... who are all looking to develop new blockbuster drugs.

From 2003 to 2008, one of the big CROs, Covance, climbed from $20 per share to $90 per share. It was a way to play the rising tide of the risky biotech sector, with a much surer outcome than buying a company betting it all on one drug.

S&A: OK... we've covered the rewards of "picks and shovels" ideas. But every investment idea has risks. What are the risks for "picks and shovels"?

Hunt: There are two major risks.

One is company-specific risk.

There is a risk the company's managers make bad decisions that reduce their competitive edge. This is where you have to do a great deal of research and know the playing field... or pay a knowledgeable industry expert to do it for you.

I think most folks should stick to the biggest and best players when looking to make "picks and shovels" investments.

The larger, more stable companies depend less on debt to conduct business. They have higher profit margins and their cash flows are more stable.

Stick with the biggest and best "picks and shovels" companies, and you add another layer of "sleep at night" safety.

The second risk is that when a sector or a commodity booms, it's eventually followed by a bust.

Most "picks and shovels" ideas should not be viewed as long-term investments. They should be viewed more as trades that can last for two, three, even five years.

For example, even the best "picks and shovels" plays in the oil industry will get hammered if oil declines by 50%. Even the best crop fertilizer producers will suffer badly if corn and soybeans enter a long-term bear market. You have to be ready to sell these investments when the market turns.

S&A: Any final words?

Hunt: One last thing... It's important to keep in mind your goals and risk tolerance as an investor.

I'm not attacking the strategy of buying riskier "one shot" exploration or production plays. You can make terrific returns by owning the "one shot" companies.

But investing and trading in these types of companies requires more specialized knowledge. They carry more risk... more than most folks are comfortable taking on.

That's why "picks and shovels" can be so useful to the conservative investor.

S&A: Thanks for joining us today.

Hunt: My pleasure.

— 6 —

'Bad to Less Bad' Trading

May 22, 2011

In this interview, Brian Hunt discusses one of the most powerful investment ideas... He calls it "the single greatest strategy on the planet."

This idea has probably created more investment fortunes than any other in history. It's a favorite of some of the world's richest and most successful investors. Yet it's so simple, even a child could understand it.

Read on to learn more about why this strategy is so powerful, and how you can use it to make money in natural resources...

Stansberry & Associates: S&A has made an art form out of "bad to less bad" trading. Can you define the term and walk us through how it works?

Brian Hunt: "Bad to less bad" is a term my colleague Steve Sjuggerud coined years ago to describe extreme contrarian trading.

It amounts to finding assets that have been hammered for some reason... be it a natural disaster, a broad market selloff, or a long industry downturn... buying them after the market has bottomed, and making tremendous returns when a bit of normalcy returns to the market – or when conditions get "less bad" for the industry.

It's the single greatest trading strategy on the planet.

S&A: Why can the gains get so big?

Hunt: When an asset suffers a major selloff... or has suffered through an extended bear market... people say things are "bad" for that asset. Nobody wants to buy it.

Mention the asset to someone at a cocktail party and they will recoil in disgust. You'd never see it on a mainstream magazine cover because the publishers know having that particular asset on their cover would gross out readers and potential newsstand buyers.

It's around this time – when most folks can't stand the thought of buying that asset – that it can start trading for less than its real, intrinsic value. It will start trading for less than its replacement value.

For example, if most folks hate a particular real estate market, houses in that market might start changing hands for well below the cost to build new ones. This is called "trading below replacement cost."

In this kind of "bad" condition, you can often buy an asset for a third or half of its book value... because nobody wants to touch it. But if you step in and buy amidst the pessimism for 50 cents on the dollar, you can double your money if just a tiny bit of optimism returns to the market and sends the asset back to its book value.

Mind you, it doesn't take great news to double the price of a cheap, hated asset... it just needs things to go from "bad to less bad."

But the great part of "bad to less bad" trading is that because of the pessimism surrounding the asset, there is little downside risk to your trade. Everyone who wanted to sell has already sold. The selling pressure is exhausted. The risk gets "wrung out" of the trade.

S&A: It sounds a lot like the famous saying from banking legend Baron Rothschild... that to make a fortune, you need to "buy when there is blood in the streets."

Hunt: Exactly. It's buying near the point of maximum pessimism.

S&A: It also sounds like the "bad" conditions can be the result of a short-term hit or the result of a long-term bear market.

Hunt: Yes. It's important to keep that aspect of "bad to less bad" trading in mind. The bad times in a particular industry could be because of a disaster, like the Gulf of Mexico blowout in 2010... or because a sector has been mired in a long bear market. Short term or long term, the main thing here is finding potential buys in assets that would make the average investor recoil in fear or disgust.

S&A: Give us an example of "bad to less bad" trading with the long-term condition in mind.

Hunt: Let's start with gold stocks.

Gold enjoyed a tremendous bull market in the 1970s... and reached a speculative peak in 1980. It then crashed and spent two decades mired in a terrible bear market. Gold fell from a peak of $800 an ounce in 1980 to around $250 in 2000.

The global economy generally did well in the '80s and '90s, so folks were much more interested in owning stocks and bonds than gold or gold stocks, which are typically seen as "safe haven" assets. They are seen as trades that do well in times of economic turmoil.

When an asset spends that many years in a bear market, folks "give up" on it. In gold's case, nobody wanted to own gold for over 15 years. Nobody wanted to invest in a gold mine for over 15 years. Most folks just wanted a hot technology stock.

There was extreme pessimism toward gold in the late 1990s and early 2000s. Everyone had sold their gold stocks. It was the definition of "bad." Many gold stocks traded for well under the replacement cost of their mines... or even worse, less than the value of the cash they held on their balance sheets.

In 2001, things started getting "less bad" in the gold business. Gold moved off its bottom of $250 per ounce and climbed 50% in just over two years. These were the early years of folks flocking toward "real assets" like gold, silver, and oil, in response to the declining U.S. dollar.

Gold advanced to $500 an ounce by 2006. It advanced to $1,000 an ounce by 2008. Gold stocks staged an incredible "bad to less bad" rally. Elite gold companies like Royal Gold and Goldcorp climbed more than 1,000% during these years. They were at depressed levels. When things got "less bad," they soared.

S&A: How about some short-term examples?

Hunt: The March 2009 panic bottom is a great example. Back then, many folks were worried we were headed for the Great Depression Part II. Credit had seized up. Stocks, real estate, bonds, and commodities had all collapsed. It wasn't just "bad" in most people's eyes. It was "horrible."

If you had stepped in and bought great stocks during this "bad" time – this time of blood running through the streets – you could have made 200% in a company like Apple in just a few years. You could have made 500% or 1,000% buying world-class resource stocks. You could have made 60% on a blue-chip company like Intel in just over a year.

Everything was depressed back then... so when things got "less bad," they shot higher like a coiled spring.

S&A: You mentioned disasters can create "bad to less bad" opportunities. Can you give us an example of this?

Hunt: Well, the Gulf of Mexico disaster of 2010 is a good example I mentioned earlier.

It was a horrible situation with the worst headlines an oil company could imagine. People died when the rig blew up. Thousands of barrels of oil were spilling into the gulf every day. The containment efforts were ineffective.

The market's reaction to the whole thing was to hammer the share prices of many of the world's best oil-producing and -drilling companies. Even companies with modest business exposure to a drilling moratorium fell 50% in just a few months.

BP, the majority owner of the well, fell 55%. Transocean, the drilling company that owned the rig, fell more than 50%. Drilling companies started selling for discounts to their book values... or absurdly cheap earnings multiples... like four or five times earnings. It was a "bad" situation.

But for investors and traders who know "bad to less bad" trading, it was an opportunity to buy great companies at discounted prices. Transocean rallied 90% off its bottom. BP rallied 80%. Again, these stocks were so deeply depressed by all of the negativity, they were like coiled springs... ready to shoot higher when things got just a little "less bad."

S&A: It's important to emphasize you're not saying you make the biggest gains as things go from "bad to good"... but "bad to less bad."

Hunt: Exactly. Steve Sjuggerud really drives this point home. He points out that you make the really extraordinary gains just when a glimmer of light appears. Not when the whole sun comes out.

You have to be willing to get in there and buy when it feels uncomfortable. If you wait until the news gets rosy and people realize it isn't the end of the world, you're going to be too late. You're going to miss out on the big, easy, early gains. You have to buy near the point of maximum pessimism.

Just thinking about buying something in a "bad" condition might make you feel sick to your stomach. But the seasoned trader knows that feeling is often a great buy signal.

S&A: It sounds like the danger here is buying something that's "bad," and watching it get "worse."

Hunt: Yes... that's the biggest risk with this idea. A bad situation *can* get much worse. You can reduce the risk of loss with two things: Waiting on a bit of price confirmation, and using stop losses.

When I say "price confirmation," I mean that I like to see the price move just a little bit in the "less bad" direction. A plunging asset is like a falling safe. If you try to catch it in the air, you'll get crushed. It's best to wait for the safe to hit the ground.

I like to see the prices slam to a bottom... then move just a bit higher from their lows. Maybe it's waiting to see a 5% move off the lows... or maybe it's waiting for the asset to reach a two-week high... or cross above a moving average. The key is waiting for the price to "confirm" your trading idea. This reduces the risk that you're buying something in free-fall.

When it comes to "bad to less bad" trading on longer-term ideas – the buying of assets that have been in long bear markets – you also want to see some sort of catalyst on the horizon that will cause the bear market to end.

For example, the catalyst that caused gold to emerge from its bear market was a big decline in the value of paper currencies... and emerging buying power from Asian countries like China and India. You want a catalyst on the horizon to ensure you're not buying an asset that will just sit there and do nothing.

The other thing when trading "bad to less bad" situations is to use a stop loss. This is a predetermined point at which you will sell a position if it moves against you.

Nobody is right on "bad to less bad" opportunities all of the time... and using a stop loss ensures that you have a plan in place to deal with adverse conditions... and that over a lifetime of trading "bad to less bad," you make a lot of money when you are right, and lose a little bit of money when you are wrong.

S&A: Thanks, Brian.

Hunt: You're welcome.

How to Be a 'Connoisseur of Extremes'

January 20, 2013

In our final interview, Brian Hunt shares a strategy he has used again and again to make consistent, low-risk profits.

Once you really understand this strategy, you'll find yourself profiting from situations where most investors take losses. It's essential reading for natural resource speculators...

———————●———————

Stansberry & Associates: You've mentioned in the past that to enjoy a lifetime of trading success, you've got to be able to spot "extremes" in the market... that you must become a "connoisseur of extremes."

What do you mean by that?

Brian Hunt: By saying you should become a "connoisseur of extremes," I'm saying you should always be searching for situations where a market is in a drastically different state than normal.

By locating these extreme states – and then betting on conditions returning in the direction of normal – you can consistently make low-risk profits in any type of market.

It's important to realize that extremes can occur in any market – from stocks to commodities to real estate to bonds to currencies.

Extremes can be fundamental in nature... like how cheap or how expensive a stock market is. Another name for this is a "valuation" extreme. Extremes can also be price-action-based... like how overbought or oversold a market is. That's a "technical" extreme. And extremes can show up in sentiment readings, like surveys that monitor investor pessimism and optimism.

S&A: Let's cover valuation extremes...

Hunt: Sure. A good example of a fundamental valuation extreme came in U.S. stocks in 1982. Back then, stocks became extremely cheap relative to their earnings power.

For U.S. stocks, the normal price-to-earnings multiple over the past hundred years or so is 16. In 1982, the economy and the stock market had been doing so poorly for so long that people simply gave up on stocks. Since nobody wanted to own stocks, they became extremely cheap. The price-to-earnings multiple fell to around 8.

It was one of the greatest times ever to buy U.S. stocks. The market rose 50% in just one year. It doubled by 1986. It rose more than 10-fold over the next 17 years.

Fast-forward about two decades and you find the opposite extreme. In 1999, optimism toward stocks was so high that the market reached a price-to-earnings ratio of 33. This was a ridiculous, extreme level of overvaluation.

Remember, the normal price-to-earnings ratio of the past 100 years is around 16. The extreme level of overvaluation made it a terrible time to buy stocks. The market crashed for several years after hitting that extreme.

When it comes to fundamentals, you need to study an asset's historical valuation and find out what's normal for that asset. When an asset gets very cheap relative to its historical valuation, you need to consider buying. When an asset gets extremely expensive relative to its historical valuation, you want to consider avoiding it... or even betting on it falling.

This goes for oil stocks, tech stocks, real estate, and lots of other assets.

S&A: OK... so people need to buy stocks when they get extremely cheap relative to their historical norm, and avoid them when they get extremely expensive relative to their historical norm. How about extremes that are "technical" in nature?

Hunt: Before we get into particulars, let's define the term to prevent confusion.

Technical analysis is the study of price action and trading volume. Many people think technical analysis is all about predicting the market, but it's not. It simply comes down to using price and volume data to gauge market action... and to help guide decisions. That's it.

There are dozens of technical indicators that measure a stock's oversold/overbought levels. One I've found useful is the "RSI," which stands for "relative strength index." The RSI is nothing magical or predictive. It's simply an objective way to gauge the overbought/oversold nature of a stock.

My colleague Jeff Clark is amazing at finding short-term technical extremes in the market. He uses an indicator called the "bullish percent index" to identify overbought/oversold extremes in broad market sectors. I'm sure Jeff will tell you there's nothing magical or predictive about the bullish percent index. Again, it's simply an objective way to gauge price action.

We are using these gauges to identify extremes in the market… then betting on the conditions being "relieved" in the other direction. When the pressure behind an extreme is released, the market tends to snap back like a rubber band stretched to its limit.

There are literally hundreds of technical indicators and chart patterns people use. While I have a handful of things that I know work, what works for me or you or someone else isn't as important as knowing the overarching goal: That you're using this stuff to spot extremes and trade them.

For example, I often trade short-term moves in blue-chip stocks, like Coke and McDonald's. These are elite businesses with tremendous competitive advantages and long histories of treating shareholders well.

But like any business, even stable blue chips go through rough patches. If they report a weak quarter or have a product recall, or any other of a dozen solvable problems, the market tends to overreact and sell the shares. The stock price will reach a state we can term "oversold." This is a condition where the stock has reached an extreme level of poor short-term price action.

It's around this time that I'll step in and trade the stock from the long side. World-class businesses have a way of rebounding from short-term setbacks. They tend to snap back from extremely oversold levels.

S&A: OK, when it comes to technical analysis, we're looking for extreme conditions that when relieved, produce "snap back" moves.

You mentioned extremes in sentiment. Let's cover that idea…

Hunt: Let's also define this term to prevent confusion. The study of market sentiment comes down to gauging the amount of pessimism or optimism toward a given asset. You can gauge the sentiment for just about any kind of asset… be it stocks, commodities, real estate, or currencies.

Gauging market sentiment is more art than science. There are lots of ways to gauge sentiment that cannot precisely be measured… and some that can.

Whatever gauges you use, the goal is the same: to find extreme levels of pessimism or optimism. You want to find situations where the majority of market participants are extremely bullish or bearish… and then bet against them. You want to go against the crowd.

When most folks can't stand the thought of owning a particular kind of investment, chances are good that it's cheap… and that it's due for at least a short-term rebound.

On the other hand, when everyone loves an asset – like when everyone loved stocks in 1999 – chances are good that the asset is expensive and due for at least a short-term drop.

A few informal sentiment gauges – the kind that can't be precisely measured – are magazine covers and cocktail party chatter.

If a mainstream publication like *Newsweek* or *Time* has an asset on its cover, chances are good that the asset is far too popular, far too expensive, and due for at least a short-term drop.

Magazine publishers have to write stories lots of people want to read. Plus, it's mostly journalists – not great investors – who write those stories. Mainstream magazines are just going to write about what's popular so they can sell lots of magazines.

Back in 1999 and 2000, they always had stocks on their covers. It was a danger sign. In 2006, it was all about how to cash in on the real estate boom. That was a danger sign.

The idea behind studying cocktail party chatter is similar. It's another way to get a feel for what the general public thinks about a given investment.

You can get a feel for this by talking to people at cocktail parties, family gatherings, holiday parties, and dinner parties. When lots of people are excited about a given asset and are buying as much as they can, it's a major warning sign. It's a sign the asset is too popular, too expensive, and due for a fall.

On the other hand, when most folks can't stand the thought of owning a given asset, chances are good that it's a good buy.

For example, back in 2003, I put a large portion of my net worth in gold. When I'd tell people that I owned a lot of gold, they'd look at me like I was crazy. You could say there was an extreme amount of disinterest in gold. Gold went on to rise many hundreds of percent.

S&A: What are some sentiment indicators that can be measured precisely?

Hunt: Money managers and investment newsletter writers are always being surveyed and monitored.

Just like most regular investors, the supposed professional investors get swept up in crowd-following behavior. You want to bet against extremes here as well.

S&A: It sounds like being a "connoisseur of extremes" is all about finding abnormal situations, and then betting on them becoming normal again.

Hunt: Exactly. It's important to note that being a "connoisseur of extremes" – and trading them – is about getting a powerful force of nature to work in your favor. That force is called "reversion to the mean."

"Reversion to the mean" is a broad term that is used to describe the tendency for things in extreme, or abnormal, states to return to more normal states. You see "reversion to the mean" all the time. You see it in academics, business, trading, and dozens of other areas.

For example, winning an NFL Super Bowl requires an extreme set of circumstances. A football team has to have a great coach... a great set of players... and has to play extremely well for an extended period of time. Its elite players have to avoid injury. It has to beat a series of excellent teams at the end of the season.

It's really hard to get all the stars aligned and pull off a Super Bowl winning season. That's why Super Bowl winners tend not to win the championship the next year. They tend to "revert to the mean" and not win it.

To go back to the example of trading extremely oversold blue-chip stocks, if a blue-chip stock like Coca-Cola is sold heavily day after day for several weeks, chances are good that its trading action will "revert to the mean" and cease being so extreme. Chances are good that it will stop falling and start rising.

S&A: Understood. Any final thoughts?

Hunt: One last thing that I think is important to note is that an extreme in valuation is often accompanied by extreme technical and sentiment readings.

That's why I believe studying and trading the market with "just" fundamentals or "just" technicals can be a limiting mindset. Consider what happened with offshore drilling stocks in mid-2010, just after the terrible Gulf of Mexico oil well disaster.

After the disaster, investors dumped shares of offshore drilling stocks. They completely overreacted. It was like people believed we'd never be drilling for oil again. Sentiment toward the sector was terrible. Even companies with little business exposure to the Gulf of Mexico fell more than 30%.

This big decline left the whole sector in an extremely oversold state. It also made the stocks very cheap. Great drilling businesses were sold down to valuations of around five times earnings.

After the selloff, you had a sector that was extremely unpopular, extremely cheap, and extremely oversold from a technical standpoint. So I went long offshore drilling stocks and made big returns in a short amount of time.

The stocks enjoyed a sharp "snapback" rally. Again, this rally was preceded by "extreme" valuation, technical, and sentiment readings.

S&A: That's why it pays to look for extremes of all types.

Hunt: Yes, exactly.

S&A: Thanks for your time.

Hunt: My pleasure.

APPENDIX:
Recommended Reading

- *Hot Commodities*
  By Jim Rogers

  The master, Jim Rogers, on the basics of commodity investing and his favorite ways to play the commodity boom. It's an older book... but full of quality information.

- *Gold: The Once and Future Money*
  By Nathan Lewis

  A great book on the history of gold and its use as money.

- *The Power of Gold*
  By Peter Bernstein

  A great history of gold and mankind's lust for it.

- *The Prize: The Epic Quest for Oil, Money & Power*
  By Daniel Yergin

  An incredible history of oil. Full of neat stories and facts. Daniel Yergin achieved something great by writing this book.

- *The Quest: Energy, Security, and the Remaking of the Modern World*
  By Daniel Yergin

  This is another brilliant book by Daniel Yergin. It continues the story he began in *The Prize*. It lays out the future of energy.

- ***Market Wizards***
  By Jack Schwager

  Interviews with the best traders and investors in the world. This book isn't focused on natural resources, but it has plenty of useful information for natural resource speculators. Make sure to read the Paul Tudor Jones interview many times.

- ***Reminiscences of a Stock Operator***
  By Edwin Lefèvre

  At his height in the 1920s, Jesse Livermore was one of the biggest traders in the world. This account of Livermore making and losing huge fortunes contains the commandments of speculation. It's not focused on natural resources, but has plenty of important insights for speculators.

If You're Interested in Learning More...

If you're interested in learning more secrets of the natural resource market, you can follow Matt Badiali's recommendations in the *S&A Resource Report.*

Since joining Stansberry & Associates in 2005, Matt has traveled the world to find the best energy and commodity-related investment ideas for his subscribers. His work has taken him to Papua New Guinea, Vancouver, Hong Kong, Texas, the Canadian Yukon, Haiti, Turkey, Nevada, Switzerland, and Kurdistan.

Every month, Matt uses this "boots on the ground" expertise and industry connections to recommend the most promising small oil and mineral explorers, drilling-service providers, power companies, and the best gold and metals companies in the world.

Matt counts many mining and energy industry veterans among his subscribers. As Gerald Wilson, director of an NYSE-listed exploration and production company, said...

> Your letter, in many instances, has confirmed good ideas under consideration and at other times introduced new ideas, which have proven to be very profitable! I look forward to your report each month and find it extremely valuable.

Learn how to access the *S&A Resource Report* by going here: www.sbry.co/Kxx7I8.

More from Stansberry & Associates

The World's Greatest Investment Ideas

The S&A Trader's Manual

The Doctor's Protocol Field Manual

High Income Retirement:
How to Safely Earn 12% to 20% Income Streams on Your Savings

World Dominating Dividend Growers:
Income Streams That Never Go Down